Better Off Wed?

Fling or Ring—
How to Know Which
Finger to Give Him

alison james

Polka Dot Press
Avon, Massachusetts

Published by
Polka Dot Press,
an imprint of Adams Media, an F+W Publications Company
57 Littlefield Street
Avon, MA 02322
www.adamsmedia.com

ISBN: 1-59337-347-3

Printed in the United States of America.

J I H G F E D C B A

Library of Congress Cataloging-in-Publication Data
James, Alison.
Better off wed? : fling or ring : how to know which finger to give him /
Alison James.
p.   cm.
ISBN 1-59337-347-3
1. Man-woman relationships. 2. Mate selection.
3. Single women—Psychology. I. Title.
HQ801.J276 2006
306.7—dc22
2005021884

This publication is designed to provide accurate and authoritative information with regard to the subject matter covered. It is sold with the understanding that the publisher is not engaged in rendering legal, accounting, or other
professional advice. If legal advice or other expert assistance is required, the
services of a competent professional person should be sought.
                    —From a *Declaration of Principles* jointly adopted by a
                         Committee of the American Bar Association and
                            a Committee of Publishers and Associations

Many of the designations used by manufacturers and sellers to distinguish
their product are claimed as trademarks. Where those designations appear in
this book and Adams Media was aware of a trademark claim, the designations
have been printed with initial capital letters.

This book is available at quantity discounts for bulk purchases.
For information, please call 1-800-872-5627.

to vanessa and tina

contents

Introduction
ix

Chapter One
You Just Know . . . or Do You?
1

Chapter Two
Dare to Compare
(Is There Someone Better out There?)
35

Chapter Three
The Real Thing, Baby
57

Chapter Four
Conflicts of Interest
81

Chapter Five
Just the Two of Us
111

Chapter Six
Who Is This Guy?
133

Chapter Seven
The Single Self
155

Chapter Eight
The Right Fit
177

Chapter Nine
The Committing Kind
199

Chapter Ten
Go Ahead . . . Flash That Finger
219

Conclusion
237

References
239

Index
241

Acknowledgments

I would like to thank Danielle Chiotti for her patience, invaluable feedback, and faith in my work; Gary Krebs, Beth Gissinger, Karen Cooper, Kirsten Amann, and the entire Adams Media sales, publicity, and editorial crew for their dedication to putting together fantastic books. I would also like to thank Bruce Vinokour for his time and assistance. My sincerest appreciation goes out to everyone who supports and contributes to my work including Shirley and Joseph Hovancik, Vanessa & Tony Shuba, Tina, Jesse and Patrick Reno, Kate Brame, Colette Curran, Liz Leo, Art Vomvas, Thomas Howe, and Lisa Huffman. Last but not least, my genuine appreciation goes out to all of those women and men who have contributed their opinions, comments, and heartfelt stories to this book.

A lasting relationship is not based on one choice you make at one point in time. It is made up of a series of choices, choices that you make every day to remain committed to the love that you're building.

ANONYMOUS

Introduction

If you were like most kids, you grew up on heavy doses of fairy tales, sappy love songs, and uplifting after-school specials. Of course, your parents did something dysfunctional along the way—your mother added water to the salad dressing to make it last longer, or your father hinted that you look fat in bulky sweaters. But aside from these little parental muck-ups, life was probably chock full of happy-go-lucky messages influential enough to keep you dotting your *i*'s with hearts for a decade or more. So when your parents or your favorite siblings said things like "Some day the right guy will sweep you off your feet" or "You have to kiss a lot of frogs before you meet your prince," you believed them. Isn't it just a matter of time before every woman meets the right guy, falls in love, and lives happily ever after?

When guys first begin to surpass us in height and we notice them for a reason other than their bowl cuts, we are rightfully excited about dating and marrying a man. We're pretty sure this love thing is just something that happens to everyone and it will happen to us too. We see couples with problems, hear men and women complain about each other, and know plenty of divorcees (maybe even our own parents), but we're certain they just didn't meet the right person. Simply put, they haven't found "The One." ("The One" must be said loudly and with force as if accompanied by thunder from the heavens. If it's sunny outside, soft harp music will do.)

"The One" is the person you'll connect with who will bring utter bliss and enchantment to your life. He's the guy who will show up on your doorstep carrying your favorite flowers, ask you to marry him in iambic pentameter verse, and then live as your handsome servant for years to come. Oh, and he'll also love your father's favorite sports team, think the hair on your upper lip is cute, and never in a million years drink the last drop of coffee on the day of your big interview.

When we start dating, we're certain that someday we will meet this illustrious, flawless, life-changing "One," and when we do, music will play or a ray of light will appear and tell us unequivocally that he is the right guy. So we date and we wait for that sign, and we do meet him—sort of. We meet a man we love, but unlike the guy we thought we'd meet, he isn't quite so perfect. He's life changing, but not always in the ways we expected. And we think maybe the music played, but we aren't 100 percent sure. So we ask, "Is this really it? What if there's something better out there? How much work should a relationship be? Does anybody ever really "just know" if he's "The One"?

Better Off Wed? will help you answer these questions and more. This guide will help you explore your biggest doubts and most complicated feelings about the guy you're dating. Based on comments and insights from thousands of women in happy, lasting relationships, you'll learn which issues really matter and which ones don't. You'll come to understand why even the best relationships can be clumsy and unpredictable. They don't always start out with a rescue from a tower and unfold with a million-dollar wedding. But that doesn't mean these couples don't live happily ever after. Many of them do—and you can too.

chapter one

You Just Know . . .

or Do You?

How do you know when you meet "The One"? Ask that question in a crowded room and at least one smug couple will eagerly chime in, "You just know!" So there you have it—see how simple it is? The story goes like this: a guy and a girl bump into each other at the deli counter, cupid appears and hits them both in the head with an arrow, and they skip off into the sunset, arm in arm. That's how real love begins, right?

Take a minute and make a list of how many couples you know who have had such a smooth start on the road to happily ever after. Not a very long list, is it? So why are we so caught up in this notion of the perfect beginning? Is it really a good indicator of how the relationship will unfold?

If you are second-guessing your guy because you weren't knocked off your feet the first time you met him, read on. If you know you love him but your feelings of utter passion are starting to wane, read on. It's time to understand what "love at first sight" really is and to determine how much of a role it plays in successful relationships.

Love at First Sight

Your idea of what it means to meet "The One" was probably cemented at an early age while watching Looney Tunes on a Saturday morning. You saw Pepé Le Pew lock eyes with a gorgeous female skunk and fall into a trance. This love scene is a familiar one in our culture, played out time and again in classic plays like Shakespeare's *Romeo and Juliet,* children's tales like *Cinderella*, and blockbuster films like *Titanic* and *Serendipity.* By the time we're old enough to date, the idea of love at first sight is ingrained in our brain. So we wait anxiously for it to happen to us, for a guy to walk by, knock us off our feet, and bring us a lifetime of happiness.

Instant Attraction

Hundreds of guys can come into and out of your life, but every now and then, one walks into the room and before you even know his name, you're sure he's simply fabulous. From the moment you see his face, you can't focus on anything but him. You're overcome with a rush of energy that's better than chocolate, better than sleep, better than a big overdose of laughing gas at the dentist. This rush is the feeling we call love at first sight. It's human nature to make snap judgments.

Studies show that people fall for each other within the first few minutes of talking. But most of us don't need research to point out this truth. We know we're attracted to some people pretty quickly and not to others. The real question is, "Once we've met him and we're attracted to him, what happens next?"

Our yearning for Hollywood romance leads us to believe that when two people fall for each other instantly, the meeting is followed by an intense, lasting connection unaffected by time, distance, or even monstrous villains with magical powers. We are hardwired to believe that love at first sight is a sign of destiny, a divine indication that we've met "The One." Modern romantics call this person a soul mate, the individual put on earth for you and you alone. This all sounds good in theory, right? But in practice, true love is just a tad more complicated.

Do you believe in love at first sight or do I have to do another walk-by?

ANONYMOUS

The "Smart Folks" Weigh In

In real life, the two of you can be completely enamored with one another and still not be the right fit for the long haul. No matter how much you love each other, he won't always be so eager to give you a back rub and make you dinner. You won't always find his snort-laugh amusing. Experts have plenty of evidence contradicting the notion that love at first sight is a good predictor of the long-term success of a relationship.

the findings Research findings on love at first sight can be as confusing as the notion itself. Use this "expert translator" to make some sense out of these insights. Then think about what they might mean for your own relationship.

Researcher According to researchers Shanhong Luo, and Eva C. Klohen at the University of Iowa, personality similarities have a strong influence on marital happiness but it takes time to know the other person well enough to understand his personality.

In Other Words Love at first sight can be misleading. You really don't know anything about the dude when you first meet him except that he isn't in jail at the moment.

Researcher Cindy Hazen, a Cornell University psychologist, has found that this feeling of love at first sight, or passion, is a biological reaction that exists solely for the purpose of encouraging us to reproduce. It wears off in eighteen to thirty months.

In Other Words The physical attraction is exciting at first, but if that's the only thing holding you together, you probably won't like each other for long.

Researcher According to a study conducted by Donatella Marazziti and Domenico Canaleb at the University of Pisa in Italy, the brain releases chemicals that cause a positive sensation we interpret as love at first sight. These chemicals are similar to stress hormones.

In Other Words What you're interpreting as a divine sign is really your body chemistry going haywire.

Researcher C. Neil MaCrae at Dartmouth University and his colleagues conducted a study that found that women express preference for masculine faces and features when they are at a more fertile time in their menstrual cycle. Feelings of attraction are strongly linked to biological processes.

In Other Words The physical attraction you feel is not very reliable. Your relationship has to be based on something more if you want it to last.

Researcher Ken Potts, a pastoral counselor and marriage and family therapist, has learned that "Initial attraction or infatuation can bring people together, but it doesn't necessarily keep them together. Healthy marriages, in fact, seem to be a complex mix of both romance and friendship."

In Other Words Finding the right guy is not as simple as locking eyes with a hunk across a crowded room.

Researcher Dr. Ted Huston, Professor of Psychology and Human Ecology at the University of Texas at Austin has discovered that after two years of marriage, less ardent lovers are just as happy as those who report love at first sight.

In Other Words You can have a happy, satisfying, long-term relationship with a guy even if you didn't feel head over heels in love when you first met him.

These experts give us plenty of reason to believe that this life-changing attraction might not be so life-changing after all. But it doesn't take a scientist to convince us that the guy we're obsessed with doesn't always turn out to be a perfect long-term fit. We can draw from our own personal memories and experiences and arrive at the same conclusion.

Too Many Dives into the Jerk Pool

We've all known some men that we just adored . . . for a few days or maybe even a month. Then Mr. Wonderful begins to grate on our nerves. He comes over looking like someone beat him with the ugly stick and drinks the last drop of orange juice straight from the carton. He's just not the suave, considerate man we thought he was—at first sight.

We've all had our fair share of experiences with love at first sight gone awry. Take a stroll down memory lane with the guys you once thought you might marry that now make you cringe.

- THE ELUSIVE CRUSH—the cute guy you fantasized about from afar for months only to meet him and discover that he liked to play with his sister's Barbies.
- THE HIMBO (MALE BIMBO)—the adorable yet clueless guy you dated until you realized you could never introduce him to your parents.
- THE HIGH SCHOOL SWEETHEART—you thought his break dancing was so cute back then, but it wasn't as appealing at your high school reunion.
- THE CHEATING ASS—he declared his undying love for you, then cheated on you with every lame girl in town.
- THE CELEBRITY GUY—he seemed more attractive before you really knew him simply because everyone else thought he was cute.
- THE NIGHT CLUB DUDE—You danced with him all night long only to discover he was heinous when the lights came on.

> I felt an instant connection with this guy and couldn't stop thinking about him for the entire first week after we met. I was positive he was the right guy for me. We went on three dates and he never called me again.
>
> —SARAH, AGE 28

Real-life Beginnings

Sometimes people do fall for each other immediately and the relationship grows into something wonderful. Other times, it starts out steamy and turns into a total disaster. And furthermore, sometimes love at first sight isn't present at all when people meet and yet they end up happily married for sixty years. So what does it really feel like to meet "The One"? Is there some absolute way to "just know"? Here's what real women have to say.

big screen love

We easily accept the fact that celebrities look larger than life on screen, but for some reason, we cannot accept the fact that Hollywood love stories are romanticized versions of the real thing. When you're dating a guy, remind yourself that love is more difficult and less glamorous than it appears in the movies. Don't compare your real relationship to made-up ones.

- "'The One' has the right mix of looks, personality, sex appeal, intelligence, and humor. The problem is, I don't really know what the right mix is."—*Samantha, age 22*
- "You know you've met the right guy when you both genuinely care for each other's well-being. Sometimes the guys we lust after most are the ones that don't give a crap if we live or die."—*Beth, age 37*
- "Laughter is what really makes a couple click and you don't laugh together until you've known each other for a while."—*Meredith, age 44*
- "The right guy for you depends on where you are in your life, what your values are, and where you see yourself going. It's not the guy who fits all thirty of your requirements; it's the one who fits your top five."—*Caitlin, age 31*
- "If you could be stuck in a boat in the middle of the ocean with him for days and never run out of things to talk about, you know he's right."—*Kara, age 25*

Meeting "The One," the guy you'll spend the rest of your life with, can feel any number of ways. There isn't one feeling that you can point to and say, "That's it. That's what it's like to meet the man of your dreams." It might pan out one way for you and a totally different way for your best friend. Some couples start out as friends. Some can't stand each other when they first meet. Others knew each other for years before recognizing they met their match.

There is no one formula or answer. All of these first meetings are right in their own way—from all of them a lifelong love can grow.

He Grew on Me

Some women don't experience that strong initial attraction upon meeting the guy they fall in love with. Rather, he won them over after several meetings or encounters. Though he didn't appeal to them at first on a physical level, as they got to know him, they started finding him attractive.

Physical attraction can grow for many reasons. You might feel more attracted to a guy after he expresses his love to you. Sometimes knowing someone love us makes us more open to the relationship. You might find a guy more physically attractive only after you learn about other qualities he brings to the table, like dependability, compassion, and even earning potential. Likewise, a guy who seems attractive initially might become a lot less attractive when you get to know his personality.

So don't rule out your guy just because you weren't passionately in love with him at first. He might have seemed a little bit nerdy or overly eager, but many women out there felt the same way and later changed their minds. Here's what some of these women have to say:

- "He followed me around for a year in college begging me to go on a date with him. I finally gave in and now I can't imagine my life without him. I'm happier than I've ever been."—*Kristin, age 27*
- "The first six months I knew him I just considered him one of the guys in our crowd. It was really not until after I got out of a bad relationship that I started to see him with new eyes." —*Megan, age 28*

- "Our relationship has developed over time and it gets stronger with each experience we have together. The funny thing is that, at first, I didn't even notice him, and we worked down the hall from one another."—*Keri, age 33*
- "He would call me every day and say 'What about now? Will you go out with me now?' He didn't come off like a stalker. He was funny about it. So I finally just had to say yes and we've been together since."—*Tina, age 40*

When attraction grows over time, you have a chance to *really* get to know a guy as a person and a friend. You also have the chance to weed him out if he doesn't click with you on a more meaningful level. Ultimately, this intimate knowledge of his personality will provide a stronger foundation for a lasting relationship than any physical element can.

Friends Forever

Friendship is a very common way for lasting relationships to begin. And it makes sense. The basis of a happy marriage is friendship and knowledge of one another. You meet in a low-pressure situation like school or work so you have a chance to develop some of the critical components of a good relationship, like trust, compassion, and a level of comfort with sharing your real feelings. So if you've known him forever but you never had that moment when "the music played," relax. It usually doesn't play when you're in math class or a tense work meeting, but that doesn't mean it won't ever. Many women marry men they knew for years and years. Often, they were very close friends with these men before they got involved with them romantically. Here's what women in this type of situation have to say:

- "I met him my junior year of high school and we were close friends. We started to date but I broke up with him after three months to date a senior. I ran into him again ten years later and we've been inseparable since."—*Diana, age 38*
- "I must have dated every one of his friends but I would always end up talking to him about my relationship problems. One day I woke up and realized that this guy had been there for me through it all. He was the one I wanted to be with."—*Kate, age 26*
- "He helped me through the death of my father and a few other tough experiences in my life. He's always been there for me and I can't imagine my life without him in it."—*Michelle, age 29*
- "I ended up hanging out with him because he worked with my sister. I never even thought of him as a potential boyfriend but one day he asked me out. It really shocked me but then when I started thinking about it, it all made sense. We really got along great."—*Sharaine, age 32*
- "The first note he ever wrote me was written on construction paper in crayon, in first grade."—*Ashley, age 33*

Friendship often ends in love;
but love in friendship—never.

CHARLES CALEB COLTON

phone indicator When you first start dating a guy, you can learn a lot about him by what he says and does over the phone. Listen carefully. But don't just listen to his words. Take in the whole picture. You can save yourself a lot of time and trouble by opening your ears and listening.

The Drunken Message Generally, drunk dialing is pretty harmless. If he calls you occasionally when he's drunk, he's thinking about you when he's out having fun and that's a good thing. If he only calls you and wants to see you when it's 3 a.m. and he's hammered, that's another story.

The Needy Message If he calls fifty times in a day and leaves you whiny messages, he might be a little too needy. It's nice to hear him say "I can't wait to see you" once in a while, but if the tape is full, your mailbox is stuffed with love letters, and you're on a first-name basis with the florist, he might be taking his adoration a little too far.

The Obligatory Call If he sounds rushed, like he's doing something else while he's talking to you, don't call him again until he makes an effort. Sometimes guys will do their time just so they can hook up with you later. If you get the sense that he never really wants to actually talk, heed your instincts and forget about him.

Calling from the Road   If the guy is always going through a tunnel, on the train, or getting ready for takeoff when he dials your number, you have to wonder why the heck he's not bothering to contact you when he's stationary. Is he hiding a wife and kids at home? Is he just too busy to bother? Cell phone man will get really annoying after a while, so if he doesn't change, kick him good-bye.

Speaker Phone   Come on now, does he really need to have you on speaker phone when he calls you? Is he *that* important? Or has he invited ten people into his office to hear your voice. If he just wants his friends to talk to his new, cute girlfriend, then he's a good guy. If, however, he wants you to know he's sitting in his corner office, feet up, talking away, get rid of the pretentious loser.

Nothing but Text Messages   What if there are no phone calls, just a little word popping up on your phone now and then? You have to wonder why he's a man of so few words. Have you heard his voice lately? Does he sound like a normal guy? Beware of guys who only text. Chances are, you're one of many girls receiving his late-night updates.

I Thought He Was a Jerk

There are lots of women at the other extreme—they couldn't stand their guy when they first met him. Then, after getting to know him, they realized he was not at all as bothersome as they thought he was. Though we do remember our first impressions of people, they aren't always 100 percent correct. Our first impression of a guy is often based on how interested he appears to be in us, and by his body language. So if he's hanging out with a group of his friends and trying to impress them, we might wrongly conclude that he's cocky or aloof. Some men act like jerks on purpose. It's their way of flirting. They don't know how to handle their feelings or approach a woman in a positive way, so they approach her the only way they know how to—they attack. So your guy isn't necessarily the wrong one just because you wanted to slap him when you first met him. Some very successful relationships do begin this way. Women who are now in a satisfying relationship with a man they once found despicable say things like:

- "My friends and I always went to this corner bar, and he would be in the back room playing darts with his friends. He walked around like he owned the place and it really ticked me off. Now I realize he only puffs his chest out when he's drunk and it's not indicative at all of his real personality."—*Jen, age 26*
- "I got stuck hanging out with him one summer because he was friends with my friends. I really thought he was an absolute ass. He was always chasing women and talking about them like they were slabs of meat. It turned out he had a crush on me the whole

time and thought he was being a cool guy by acting that way."—
Dana, age 35

- "I had heard so much about him from friends. They talked about how he was a cocky ass, and so when I saw him, I really didn't even want to talk to him. Now even my friends admit that they were wrong. He's the nicest guy."—*Hannah, age 27*

- "He and I met when we were lawyers for opposing teams on a case five years ago. I hated his team so much for making the experience difficult. I never even dreamed I would end up dating this man. When the whole thing was over, he asked me out and the rest is history."—*Maggie, age 38*

One-Sided Love

If love at first sight is the "divine sign" that you're with the right person, why is it that in some cases, only one member of the partnership felt it? Many of these one-sided chemical attractions can develop into very committed relationships that last a lifetime. One person is simply a helpless romantic and the other takes a little bit longer to jump on the love boat. Women in relationships that started this way say things like:

- "It was instant attraction for him, but for me it sort of grew. I'm just not the type of person who is ever blinded by something. I think things through."—*Catherine, 40*

- "He said he thought I was too pretty for him. Ten years later, he's checked out by members of the opposite sex far more often than I am."—*Laurie, 38*

- "He claims I liked him more, but I always felt like I could sense that he worshiped me. Shhh. He does. He clearly worships me."
  —*Holly, 30*

No Formula

How viable is the formula of man + woman + love at first sight = successful long-term relationship? Chemical attraction is a wonderful feeling, but we need to look at it with a critical eye. We can't just assume it's the best way for a relationship to begin simply because we're told it is. Many long-term relationships that work don't start out on such a steamy note. They don't begin with a single moment of utter clarity. In fact, most lasting relationships start out with a little bit of doubt. A chemical reaction does not guarantee the success of a relationship any more than a designer label guarantees your adorable heels will get you through an arduous ten-mile hike. Likewise, the absence of that initial chemical big boom does not doom a couple to a life of boring, miserable, passionless love. Relationships begin in many different ways and all of them can lead to a fantastic lifetime of love if other important details are in place.

One Size Fits All?

All of this musing still doesn't answer the burning question, How do you know if he's "The One?" By now, you've probably surmised the true answer: there isn't just *one way to know*. A one-size-fits-all approach works well for scarves and earrings, but unfortunately, it doesn't work for love. In a world in which women are so different from one another and have so many different needs, we can't be lumped together. Finding love for life will mean something unique and special to each of us. With this fact in mind, realize that meeting "The One" might feel very different for you than it does for your best friend, your sister, or your coworker. There's no way it "should" happen, so when someone tries to tell you hands down that they know how it feels, take it with a grain of salt. You need to decide for yourself what your own experience should be, based on your personality and needs.

The Rational Thinker

Your checkbook is always balanced to the penny, your clothes are hung in your closet according to color, and your books are arranged in alphabetical order. You never make a

love 101

Many different factors added together can equal lasting love, so don't get hooked on one particular equation.

- Man + woman + friendship = lasting love
- Cute male masseuse + woman = lasting love
- Man + woman + shared goals and dreams = lasting love
- Man who likes to shoe shop + woman = lasting love
- Rich sugar daddy + woman + cute gardener = lasting love

major decision without weighing it carefully—from changing jobs to buying a car or a house. Naturally you approach love in the same way. But love isn't a problem to solve. It doesn't have one glaring right answer. It might make you feel uncomfortable. You're the Rational Thinker.

> **Your Version of Love at First Sight:** He's cute . . . but is he just right? What if our kids end up with his geeky laugh?
> **Your Question:** If this is it, why do I have so many concerns?

A woman who approaches her life in a cautious manner will probably approach her relationships that way too. To her, love is like a chemistry experiment. She analyzes it, tries to gauge the outcome, and is thrown off if an explosion occurs that she didn't predict. If this description sounds like you, recognize that you will always ask questions when you meet a guy. You will try to make all the pieces fit. Love is naturally awkward, and that fact may make it uncomfortable for you, but love is also very exciting.

> **Your Challenge:** Remember that love does not fall into neat little piles or follow a set of universal rules.

The Romantic

You cry over television commercials. You've been planning the perfect wedding since you were six. Valentine's Day is practically a holy day for you. You are in love with love and it's easy for your judgment to get a little clouded by your fairy-tale dreams.

Your Version of Love at First Sight: He's it! Love is beautiful! Let's get married tomorrow.

Your Question(s): How soon can we book the reception hall? Why do people keep asking me if I'm sure? We've already known each other for three weeks. Isn't that long enough?

If any of this sounds familiar, you are definitely the Romantic. You want the fairy tale from start to finish and you're not going to let anyone tell you that you can't have it. You drive the Rational Thinker crazy. She can't figure out how you can possibly be so sure, and you don't understand why she wants her boyfriend to have a ten-year career plan.

As the Romantic, you don't care too much about your guy's career plan or his bald spot or even the fact that you met him at a funeral. You're not going to let these little details ruin your happiness.

Your Challenge: You have to relax a little bit and let life and love happen. You can't force these things. So if your mom or your friends question your decision, don't disown them. Try to take a step back and see your situation objectively. Make sure you're not so caught up in the moment that you're forgetting about the long-term implications of your impulsive decisions.

> If music plays when you meet a guy, check to see if you're wearing headphones or if someone nearby is singing. If you can't find a logical explanation, seek professional help.
>
> ANONYMOUS

The Beautician

When you were six, you gave your Barbie dolls cool new haircuts. In high school, you made it your mission to make over all of the geeky girls into hot chicks. You take pride in your appearance and you want those around you to do the same. You're the Beautician.

Your Version of Love at First Sight: Oh, he'll be perfect after I give him a clean, close shave!

Your Question: Wouldn't I accept him "as is" if I really loved him?

When you see a cute but grungy guy, do you instantly think, "He'll scrub up well?" Do you envision the dapper Don Juan he could be instead of the goofy Don Knotts before you?

This is classic Beautician behavior. When you meet "The One," you'll see him as a project. The only music playing when you meet a guy is Madonna's "Dress You Up." And you want to start dressing him up right away—in a brand-new well-tailored suit and tie. You've even been known to pass up men who are next to perfect because there's no part of them you can fix.

Your Challenge: You're obviously a creative, motivated person. So maybe you should take up some hobbies like interior design or arts and crafts so you stop making men your project. Most guys need a little bit of clean-up when you meet them to get them just right, but make sure you're not passing up some great guys just because they don't require enough fixing. Remember that what you see when you're dating someone is what you get, for the most part. You aren't going to transform him into a gritty cowboy if he's a yuppie type. You probably won't get him to love the outdoors if he's afraid of a housefly. In the end, your fix-ups just won't last.

Most importantly, remember that sometimes the urge to fix others is a symptom of a bigger issue. Some women pick men with flaws because they are afraid of intimacy and they want an easy out. Other women feel like they need to fix something about themselves but they focus their energy on a guy instead. If any of these possibilities ring true, work on mending your own feelings before you enter into another relationship.

The Pessimist

Your glass is always half-empty. You feel like there's a huge black relationship cloud that follows you around flashing a neon sign that reads "BAD LUCK." The last guy you really liked was . . . you can't remember back that far. You're a pessimist.

Your Version of Love at First Sight: I think our eyes met but I'm pretty sure he'll dump me once he meets my sister. **Your Question:** Is he making me insecure or am I always this way?

Do you see a breakup waiting to happen every time you meet a guy you adore? Are you certain that if you like him too much, he'll dump you and sleep with your best friend? If this sounds like you, make sure you don't suffer from Settle Syndrome.

Settle Syndrome is the tendency to go for guys who are not quite worthy just because you know they are safe and they'll worship you. A pessimist wants to be sure that her guy will never surf off into the sunset with a blond bimbo at the beach. So she picks one who idolizes her even if she doesn't love him.

Your Challenge: Start giving guys you like a chance. Don't sabotage a relationship by assuming a guy's not into you at the outset. Try switching your negative thoughts around— he's lucky to have you and he should treat you as such. If you keep approaching love with a negative attitude, your Mr. Right is always going to be Mr. Maybe, the guy who needs you just a little more than you need him, the one who makes you boringly comfortable. If you settle for a guy simply because you're feeling down, you're bound to want someone different when you get your spunky self back.

The Masochist

You break up with a guy as soon as he likes you because you think you don't deserve him. You always seem to fall for men who never call you back. You love "the chase," even if it leads you up a dangerous mountain and through a burning cave. You are the Masochist.

Your Version of Love at First Sight: He hasn't called in three weeks! How adorable, right? He's playing hard to get!

Your Question: If he's too nice to me, doesn't that mean something's wrong with him?

You like a challenge, and you feel a boost in confidence when you win a prize or get a man who is sought after by other women. You find nice guys a little boring. Your idea of "The One" is the guy you have to fight for regularly, the one who is slightly mean to you.

Your Challenge: Recognize that real, lasting love takes two willing participants. If you can't get him on the phone, he probably isn't as willing as you hope he is. Try to understand why you like impossible men. Sometimes we feel a confidence boost when we win attention from a difficult person, but you don't need a guy's attention for confidence. Focus on breaking your pattern. Try to date men who are more considerate and responsive. Realize that you think aloof guys are superhuman only because you haven't spent enough time with them to see their glaring flaws.

No matter what your personality type, you can be sure that your experience with men is unique to you. Recognize that only you can decide if your guy is "The One" based on what you know about yourself and the way the two of you interact. Are you normally analytical or are you questioning this guy more than usual? Do you always fall head over heels in love or does this guy have a little extra something the others didn't have? Are you pessimistic about love, and if so, are you sure you're not underestimating your own potential to attract a worthwhile guy? Your relationships will not mirror those of other women you meet. So don't measure your experience against someone else's notion of "true love." Another person simply can't tell you what it's going to be like for you to meet "The One." You have to decide for yourself.

> What I call "the music playing," my sister refers to as "chemistry." But my mother insists the correct term is "the naiveté of youth."
>
> ANONYMOUS

Important Certainties

While you can't always "just know" you want to wake up every day for the rest of your life next to a man you met in line this morning at Starbucks, there *are* certain things you can "just know" about a guy from the start. After all, you do have instincts and the ability to read other people based on your past experiences. While you might have little doubts about a guy when you first meet him—you imagined yourself with a blond and he has dark hair, or you hate accents and he's from the UK—you can learn to push these doubts aside. There are some nagging issues, however, that you cannot ignore. Pay attention to these little things that you should "just know" when you meet a guy:

- While you might not know if he's always respectful, you do know how well he's treating you at the moment.
- While you might not know if he's a sex addict, you should be able to tell if he's already trying to get you to go back to his place for the night.
- While you might not know if he's a felon fleeing the law, you can tell if he's trying to do something illegal to you.
- While you might not be able to tell if he'll cheat on you like crazy, you can get a vibe for whether or not he's a player feeding you lines.
- While you might not know if he has any weird private fetishes, you can definitely tell if he has public ones.
- While you might not know if he has a great sense of humor, you can tell whether or not he likes to smile.
- While you might not know what's important to him in life, you can tell what he cares about in women by listening to the questions he asks you.

In other words, give the poor guy a second chance, but be smart and heed your instincts. If you think the guy is a total player, scumbag, loser, or dangerous personality, he doesn't deserve a second chance. If you get an instant urge to run in the other direction, he's definitely not right for you. But there's another side of it—if you enjoyed his company but can't get past the fact that he drank his beer through a straw, let it go this time. Give the guy a break. The music didn't play, but that might mean his radio is just temporarily broken. Sometimes you just need to adjust the speakers a little and then you'll hear it loud and clear.

> You won't know any guy completely just by looking into his eyes. In fact, I've been happily married for twenty years and I'm still discovering new things about my husband every day that scare the heck out of me.
>
> SHARON, AGE 47

The Second (or Third!) Chance

Most of us aren't sure what we want for dinner tonight, let alone whether we want to date the guy we just met a day ago. And that's okay. But if you really want to make a connection with someone, sometimes a second chance holds even more opportunity than the first did. Plenty of happily married people say things like, "My friend talked me into seeing him a second time" or "He kept calling me and finally I gave in because I figured maybe he could help me find a new job." Think about all the silly or insecure things you've done on first dates and how wrong guys would be if they judged you solely by these behaviors. We all do crazy things when our nerves get the best of us. So it's worthwhile to give the less-than-perfect guys a second chance—but which ones? Which first date behaviors are benign and which are signs you should run? If you're already in a relationship, this checklist will help you figure out if you had a good, healthy accepting attitude when you first met your guy, or if you overlooked a little bit more than you should have.

He's Cute but He's Not Exactly My Fantasy Man

Everyone has an ideal guy. Yours might be Spiderman (there's nothing like a mask and a tight butt); the fireman down the street; or a nice, clean-cut, outdoorsy boy like the camp counselor you had a crush on when you were ten. What does your fantasy man look like and how many people on this planet actually fit the description?

Still thinking?

Most great guys do not look, talk, or behave like our dream guy. In fact, most fantasy men aren't even as perfect as we imagine them to be. Once we get to know them, we find out that they have flaws too. So if you find a guy attractive but he isn't quite like the dream man you adore, give him one more chance (or two!).

My friend told me when she met her husband that she "just knew" he was "The One." I often wonder, did she "just know" they would get divorced too?

VANESSA, AGE 35

He Seems Insecure

Women are often attracted to men who appear confident. Evolutionary psychologists insist that a woman is attracted to the guy who acts like he's king of the jungle because in primitive times, women needed a strong man for protection. But modern men can't demonstrate to us that they are king of the jungle by fighting off enemies or wrestling animals to the ground for food. So today's men show their prowess in their own unique ways.

Some excel at sports. Others defend their beliefs in conversation or battle their boss for a raise. When you first meet a guy, you can't always tell how confident he truly is. He might be very self-assured once you get to know him, but timid around new people. Or he might come off as nervous on the first date because he finds you attractive. If the conversation is interesting and you enjoy his company, don't judge him right away. Give him another chance to show you how confident he can be.

His Tastes Just Don't Gel with Yours

It's important that you and your guy have similar tastes and preferences, but the way he looks on the first date can be deceiving. If he shows up dressed in black from head to toe, that doesn't mean he's a Goth guy and he'll never dress like a preppie. Maybe his fashion-conscious coworker recommended the dark ensemble and it's not his style at all.

As the relationship progresses, you'll learn so much more about each other. There will inevitably be items in his wardrobe that warrant an arrest from the fashion police. You will both have to learn to live with things you don't like about each other's tastes and preferences. But don't jump the gun and declare him a lost cause simply because his fashion sense doesn't gel with yours on the first date.

Give him a chance to show you all sides of himself before you make a decision.

> Whenever I date a guy, I think, is this the man I want my children to spend their weekends with?
>
> RITA RUDNER

He Seems Like He's Too "Something"

On the first date, a guy might not be himself in other ways too. If he's driving you nuts because he's acting too rich, too sweet, too macho, or "too" something else, but you think you might like him, go out with him again and see if he tones down his flashy flaw once he's more comfortable with you. You might find that he's still a lot of fun but not quite as overbearing as he seemed on the first date.

He Has Strange Habits

It's important that you feel some sort of bond with the person you're with on a first date, but weird things still happen and make the moment awkward. Perhaps he'll have terrible table manners. He slurps his coffee, grabs the lemon out of his mixed drink with his fingers and sucks on it, or even picks his teeth with his fork when he thinks you're not looking. While you of course want him to have impeccable manners and great charm, recognize that your major faux pas might be something his family has done at dinner every night since the day

strange first-date behaviors

When you're trying to decide if a guy is "The One," keep in mind that we've all done some wacky and ridiculous things on a first or second date. Try not to judge him for little things he might be doing simply because he's nervous or out of his element. Sometimes a force takes over and normal, desirable people do some very undesirable things.

- "I sipped the vinegar at the dinner table. I thought it was wine."—*Sidney, age 23*

- "I closed my coat in the door of the cab and it dragged in the mud until we got to the restaurant."—*Emily, age 26*

- "I tried to look extremely sexy and confident, but I was wearing heels I couldn't walk in and a shirt that made me feel naked, so I essentially waddled everywhere we went the entire night."—*Morgan, age 31*

- "I snorted a margarita up my nose when I laughed, then got a headache from the cold and had to excuse myself."—*Rosalind, age 24*

- "I was so nervous I kept knocking my utensils onto the floor and the waiter got annoyed."—*Danielle, age 26* he was born. Keep in mind that he might think it's bizarre that you ate the appetizer with your fingers, or that you laughed at a startling story you heard on the evening news. People have different ideas of acceptable dress, behavior, and manners, and while it is important that you fall within the same range of compatibility, you don't have to match perfectly and, in fact, most people don't. You can always stitch his mouth shut if he slurps his coffee one too many times.

> Lasting love is much more complicated than a moment of fireworks between two strangers. It grows, changes, molds, shapes, and stretches into something deeper, meaningful, and lasting if, and only if, both people are willing to work at it.
>
> ANONYMOUS

Quick Check

Remember that you won't always know "The One" when he's standing right in front of you or sitting across from you at a restaurant. You might have to go out with him one more time or even several more times to really know. If you're not sure whether to go on another date with a guy, ask yourself these questions:

1. Would you enjoy introducing him to your friends because you think he's funny or interesting?
2. Does he make you laugh and get your jokes?

common sales strategies When a guy wants to impress you, he'll become the ultimate salesman, showcasing his good side, even though you might not think it's so good. If he is selling himself hard on the first date and it's a little annoying but you still enjoy his company, give him a second chance. See if he keeps up his salesman routine the second time around. Check out the popular types of "salesmen":

THE WHEELER AND DEALER He's a big-shot businessman on his cell phone at dinner, talking as if he's sealing the final terms of a billion-dollar deal. He's important and he wants you to know it. You're thinking, "Um, I'm impressed."
Hope By date three, you'll learn that though his job is lucrative, he doesn't actually take himself that seriously.
Fear By date three, you'll learn that he doesn't even have a job and that he's hoping to move into your place for a while until he gets back on his feet.

THE CHARMER He tells you that you're beautiful, kisses you on the cheek, and talks like a total gentleman.
Hope He'll remain charming but won't be so sappy about it.
Fear A year into the relationship he'll be calling you "wench" and telling you to pull out your own darn chair.

THE INTELLECTUAL He talks about philosophy and knows what art exhibit is on display. He has opinions on many issues.
Hope He is smart enough to hold an interesting conversation but he'll stop trying so hard to showcase his intelligence.

Fear   He's never read the paper in his life and did a cram session right before the date to impress you.

THE COMEDIAN   He loves a good joke and wants to make you laugh. He teases you, the waitress, and the coat-check girl in the restaurant.
Hope   His corny sense of humor will evolve and by the next date he will be really funny.
Fear   He'll get increasingly tiresome and eventually he'll even steal lines from movies and claim them as his own.

MR. SOCIAL   He wants you to know that he gets along with every-body. He is the mayor of your neighborhood. When you walk into a bar with him, everyone knows his name and gives him a high five.
Hope   He is social and everyone likes him, but he likes his private time too and doesn't always need to be the center of attention.
Fear   Everyone in the bar knows him because he's been there by him-self seven nights a week for the past six months.

THE CELEBRITY   He is a friend of the Hiltons. His dad knows Donald Trump. He also has an "in" with all the royal families of Europe. He's a well-connected dude.
Hope   He values his relationships with friends. He likes to be social and he'll always help you host a good party.
Fear   He's a weirdo with a screw loose and he believes he's king of his delusional world.

THE LISTENER   He hangs on your every word. He listens intently and asks questions. Sometimes you feel like he's studying you.
Hope   He'll continue to be interested in you but he'll stop trying so hard to show it.
Fear   Six months later he won't pay attention to a damn thing you say and you'll have to scream for him to turn down the volume on his iPod.

3. Does he seem like a good, trustworthy person?
4. Did you have more fun with him than you do with your friends? Your dog?
5. Do you sort of want to see him again but you just need an extra push?
6. Is he cute enough? Can you see yourself kissing him?

If you can answer yes to all of these questions, give him a second chance.

> It is only with the heart that one can see rightly;
> what is essential is invisible to the eye.
>
> ANTOINE DE SAINT-EXUPÉRY

Love at first sight is not all it's cracked up to be, but that doesn't mean you have to give up on romance. It simply means that you might have to accept the fact that love doesn't always unfold so neatly and romance can take many forms. The right guy might walk into your life, but he also might run, jump, cartwheel, somersault, trip, or sidestep into your life. So keep your eyes and your heart open to all of the possible ways it can feel to meet "The One." And know that not every woman in this world will "just know" when she meets him.

chapter two

Dare to Compare

Is There Someone Better out There?

Some people say that when you're dating the man you're meant to spend your life with, you don't even notice other men around you. You kind of have to wonder—are they blind?

Even when you're in a great relationship, it's totally natural that you will compare your guy to coworkers, ex-boyfriends, characters in movies, and even random men on the street. After all, you're dating—not dead. We all just want some kind of proof, a measurement or rating that tells us unequivocally whether or not we're with the right guy. We think that if we get it, we'll finally have the reassurance we're looking for, and we'll be able to move forward with confidence. But can we get this kind of verification? Can comparisons to other men really give us the guarantee we're looking for? Let's explore what information we really glean when we dare to compare.

Terrible or Bearable?

Fortunately, guys are abundant on our planet. The little suckers are everywhere. In most public places if you stood with your arms straight out and twirled around, you would smack at least one in the head. So it makes sense that even when you're in a good relationship, sometimes you look at all the other options and wonder, "Is there someone better out there?" We do it with shoes, clothes, jobs, and, heck, just about everything else in life. It's human nature to compete and compare. We're not always proud of it, but we do it. So instead of worrying about the fact that you do it, stop listening to those people who say, "He's definitely wrong for you if you're looking at other men," and focus on answering the question that matters: Why? Why are you looking at other men, and what, if anything, does it mean for your relationship? Focus on figuring out if your wandering eye is a symptom of a bigger problem by answering these five questions.

Question #1
Does It Cause You Anxiety?

Does the fact that you're comparing your guy to others cause you anxiety? Are you lying in bed at night feeling as if you've cheated on your guy simply because you can't get another one out of your head? If you feel distressed because you are so captivated by someone else, it is a bright blinking sign that you are with the wrong guy. Whether the other guy is right for you or not, he is a distraction that is telling you something about the one you're with. It's very normal to think about other men and even to find them attractive. But if you're thinking about other men more than you think about your own, it's pretty clear that your anguish is not going to go away until you cut your guy loose and date one that you really want to be with. If you're still not sure whether or not you're sufficiently anxious, ask yourself:

- Do you kiss your boyfriend and feel guilty about it because your heart isn't in it?
- Do you tell people you're single when you're out at night, and then feel awful about it?
- Have you come close several times to breaking up with your boyfriend after freaking out about the fact that you're attracted to other men?
- Are you scared to death that he's going to ask you to meet his parents or propose to you because you know that you're not fully into him?

Question #2
Is It Circumstantial?

Sometimes you might compare your guy to other men when you're angry with him. If he's bugging you, you'll notice everything that's wrong with him. Then, if another guy happens to walk into the room, the new guy might seem wonderful by comparison. If you only compare your guy to others when you're in a bad mood or you're fighting with him, it's no big deal. It's normal for us to feel like the grass is greener on the other side when we're experiencing a few weeds and rough patches on our own side. If you think other men are a heck of a lot more appealing even when you and your guy are getting along great, however, it's obviously a sign that something is not right with the relationship. Here are a few other examples of comparisons you might make when your own relationship is not stellar:

- You're angry with him for calling you flabby so you compare him to guys who are more in shape than he is and point out his shortcomings.
- You bring him to your high school reunion and compare him to your high school sweetheart.
- You spend a week scuba diving and develop a mini-crush on your scuba instructor. You compare your guy to scuba man and decide he's not adventurous enough.
- You see the same cute guy in the deli every day and he's always a gentleman, allowing you to order your sandwich first. You are annoyed with your guy when you get home at night because he doesn't have manners like deli dude.

Question #3
Is It a Pattern?

Is your wandering eye a pattern? Do you constantly compare every man you date to other guys out there? Do you do this same thing in other areas of your life? For example, do you get really hung up on what designer shoes your friends have or what type of house they live in? Some women always covet what they can't have. They define their own success and happiness by how they rate against others. Now, we all do this to some extent, but most of us don't dwell on our own short-comings. We don't define our entire life by how we stack up against friends. If you are constantly comparing everything in your life to what other people have—it's not a sign that the relationship needs help; it's a sign that you might need help.

The only way you'll learn to be happy with what you have is to learn to define yourself by your own standards and not by those set by others. This isn't a "self-esteem" book, so we won't go into all the ways you can do that here, but the bottom line is that anything you can do to increase your self-confidence will help. It could mean a few good books on building confidence, therapy, or focusing on an activity in which you excel. Once you are more self-assured, you won't compare every aspect of your life—including your guy—to others. Comparing your guy to others might be a symptom of a larger problem if:

- You are always jealous of other women in every area—their looks, their jobs, their houses, or their boyfriends. Even if your outfit is great, you covet the one your friend has.
- Regardless of what guy you're with, you always end up leaving him for the next best thing.
- You have trouble remaining dedicated to one activity or job because you always feel like you're missing something better out there.
- No matter how good you look or how great your life is going, you aren't happy. There's always something you want to change or do differently.

Question #4
Does It Make You Want to Transform Your Guy?

Do you look at other men and feel like you desperately need to change your guy? We all make little requests of the man we're dating now and then, like "How about this shirt instead of your tie-dye one?" or "Why not get those eyebrows trimmed?" But if you have your eye on a guy or two that you admire, and you've decided that you are going to try to mold your guy to be just like them, you definitely have a relationship problem on your hands. You've heard it time and again and it's true—what you see is what you get when you're dating someone. He's not going to change much, if at all. So your efforts are futile. Any time another man you know is making you want to send yours to the shop for a full-body tune-up, the relationship is just not right. You are trying to change him if:

- You correct his sentences in front of other people and try to steer him in conversation.
- You "dress him up" and put him through your own personal charm school before he meets your friends because you want him to be a certain way.
- You refuse to accept the fact that he just doesn't want to wear a salmon-colored shirt to work, so you buy him three.
- You beg him to lighten his hair, darken his eyebrows, and buy a spray tan package before your friend's wedding.

Question #5
Would You Dump Your Guy If It Was Easy?

If you could get rid of your guy with no hassle, would you do it? If a new guy appeared tomorrow, one you really like, and your current boyfriend left without saying a word, no explanation required, would that make you happy? If so, you are in your relationship solely because it's comfortable. While you want to be comfortable with a man you're dating and you both want to know each other well, comfort in and of itself is not enough of a reason to continue to date someone. You can be comfortable and still not be content. You're probably comfortable with plenty of men out there—coworkers, friends, acquaintances—but that doesn't mean you want to spend the rest of your life with them. People often mistake comfort for love. You're just too accustomed to life with your boyfriend to break it off even though you know you should. You won't always recognize this situation when you're in it unless you look for the signs. Sometimes it's hard to admit to yourself that you are remaining in the relationship for the wrong reasons, that you're just too lazy to make a move. The comfort you feel is the wrong kind of comfort if:

- You can't remember a time where you were really excited to be with your boyfriend.
- You never really planned to stay with him for any length of time. You've been eyeing other guys since the beginning, waiting for the right one to come along.
- Any warm body can fulfill the needs this guy does. Deep down inside, you know that maybe you just need a cat or dog.

Measuring Mode

We all have our own standards we use to evaluate men when we're scoping them out. But sometimes when we're actually dating a guy, we have a hard time deciding if he's meeting all of our needs. We spot another appealing guy and we think, "Aha! My guy does not measure up! So I must be with the wrong person." But that's not always the case. Take some time to explore the comparisons you make and keep in mind the questions you just answered. The comparisons you make can give you insight into how you really feel about the man you're with.

Your Personal Yardstick

Write down all the instances you can think of where you used another man to size up your guy. (That sounds kind of kinky for some reason!) Do you look at your boyfriend's picture alongside a photo of your ex and feel torn? Do you listen to a friend talk about her special birthday party that her boyfriend planned and feel a little envious? Here are some of the more common benchmarks women use to size up their guy. These comparisons can be totally harmless, or signs of a bigger issue. Think about what they mean for you in your life.

The Stranger

You've seen him here and there, at work or at parties, and maybe you've even exchanged a few sentences with him. You don't really know him but you feel like you do because you've watched him walk, talk, and mix a martini. You know for sure that he's handsome and charismatic. He's a stranger, but in your mind, he's possibly "The One" who can give your boyfriend a run for his money.

Your wandering eye is no big deal if:
- You do it because you love eye candy and you've always been one to notice any cute guy in your line of sight.
- You've only checked him out a couple of times when you and your boyfriend were arguing.
- You're fully aware that there is absolutely no chance he truly is as wonderful as your mind has made him out to be.

It is cause for concern if:
- You feel a sinking pit in your stomach when you hear Mr. Stranger is dating someone else. You should be thinking of it as a sign that he *isn't* right for you, not as an opportunity you missed.
- You change your routine regularly to try to run into him, make conversation with him, or work with him on projects.
- You know you would definitely break up with your boyfriend if this guy asked you out.

Many a dangerous temptation comes to us in fine gay colors that are but skin-deep.

MATHEW HENRY

The Rescuer

He's a megamillionaire you met at a party. You can't stop thinking about him and what a wonderful lifestyle you would have if you married him. You would get to travel the world; eat at the finest restaurants; and hire a maid, a gardener, and a personal masseuse. You would never have to work or worry about money again. Even if he's not rich, maybe he's exciting in a way that your current boyfriend is not. He is a rescuer because he will help you escape your current humdrum lifestyle and whisk you away to one that is infinitely more appealing.

Your fantasy is no big deal if:
- Thoughts of him are fleeting and usually correlate with the arrival of your credit card statement.
- Your daydream is always interrupted by those things about him you can't stand, like the fact that he doesn't get your sense of humor or that the two of you have nothing in common.
- You realize that you think about him because you find his lifestyle motivating. He makes you want to work harder, make more money, or start your own business.

It is cause for concern if:
- He would still interest you if you won $10 million in the lottery. In other words, you would find him appealing even if you could achieve the lifestyle you want in some other way.
- Thoughts of him make you resent your boyfriend.
- Seeing this guy makes you realize that you haven't lived enough or that you've missed out on opportunities in life and it's because your boyfriend is holding you back.

The Ex-Boyfriend

You thought you were over your ex but now you aren't so sure. You recently found a shoebox under your bed full of photos of him and while your guy was out, you took a stroll down memory lane. You're also on your ex's e-mail distribution list so you know he just moved back to your neighborhood. You wonder, "Would he possibly be the best match for me after all? Did I make a terrible mistake?" You remember all the fun the two of you had together and you can't help but compare your current boyfriend to him and notice the ways your beau doesn't measure up.

A walk down memory lane is no big deal if:
- You miss him for a day or two, but then forget about him and refocus on the great guy you're with right now.
- You realize that you don't really miss him; you miss the time when the two of you dated. He reminds you of the good old days and makes you long to go back.
- You find the bad picture of him beneath all the good ones and remember what it is about him that you didn't like.

It is cause for concern if:
- You realize that you've never been happy with your current boyfriend like you were with your ex.
- You have no qualms about calling him up and going out with him behind your boyfriend's back.
- Your interest in your ex lasts more than just a few days. You still can't stop thinking about how you lost the best thing that ever happened to you.

Her Boyfriend

She is your best friend, so you don't want to find her boyfriend appealing, but you can't help it.

He is so sweet to her, always attentive and kind.

He hangs on her every word.

You get a holiday card from them and it has a picture of the two of them on it looking cheery and in love. In the only "couple" photo you have, you look like a deer caught in headlights.

You can't help but wonder if maybe you're settling. After all, you and your boyfriend argue sometimes and he didn't even want to send out holiday cards.

Your interest is no big deal if:

- You mull over your feelings and realize that her boyfriend would never be right for you. Despite all the wonderful things he does, he just doesn't measure up to your beau in the areas that matter.

- She's trying extra hard to make her relationship seem perfect by rubbing their "happiness" in your face. The two of you have always had antagonistic moments and you compete in almost everything.

- Your guy steps up to the plate in the ways that really matter. If watching your friend's relationship really does highlight a problem in your own, your guy is willing to work with you to fix that problem.

It is cause for concern if:

- You spend endless energy trying to make your boyfriend be more like hers.
- You have an aching feeling in your stomach every time you see your friend's boyfriend because it reminds you that yours isn't everything you want him to be.
- You feel like many other women you know have a better boyfriend than you do. You are constantly surprised to hear stories of how sweet, caring, or loyal their boyfriends are.

i'll have what she's having

Are you envious of another woman because her love life seems so perfect? Try to remember that every relationship has its problems. If you had all of the little nuggets of private information at your disposal, you would discover things like:

- She's spent every day since she married him trying to increase his coordination because he trips over his own two feet.
- She has a secret crush on your boyfriend.
- He's not always as nicey-nicey as he puts on in public. In fact, he likes to call her "Fatty" whenever she eats ice cream, and he leaves diet literature under her pillow.
- They almost broke up a dozen times the first year they met.
- She has come close to flushing the remote control down the toilet to get him to stop watching television.
- She wishes he would listen to her more often. What?

The Bosom Buddy

You met him your sophomore year and the two of you have been best friends since. You've traveled together, met each other's parents, and now you still talk on the phone once a week. He's just a guy who "gets" you and sometimes you wonder if maybe, just maybe, you are supposed to end up with him. You have days when you aren't sure your boyfriend will ever be as good a friend as your longtime buddy.

Being fond of a guy friend is no big deal if:
- The idea of being romantically involved with him usually only crosses your mind when you're fighting with your own guy. Heck, you used to adore your friend's mother when you were fighting with your own, but that didn't mean you wanted to run away from home.
- You realize that regardless of how much you do have in common with your buddy, he has certain qualities that just aren't what you are looking for in a long-term partner.
- Your thoughts of your buddy quickly sour when you imagine interacting with him physically.

It is cause for concern if:
- You can talk to your buddy about your feelings or issues in your life that your boyfriend ignores.
- Your buddy is there for you when you're in distress and your boyfriend is not.
- You have much more fun when your buddy tags along to movies, parties, or even dinner with you and your boyfriend.

Chances are, not all the men you use to size up your guy are listed here. So think about your own life and the men who intrigue you. Some of them will be guys you've thought about once or twice and then forgotten. Others, however, might be indicators of a bigger problem in your relationship. Remember, comparing your boyfriend to other men doesn't necessarily mean your relationship is bad. What really matters is "Why?"

If you think about these men and decide that you really do love your guy, you've passed an important test. You have proven that you can remain committed to him despite temptation around you. But remember, other men are not going to go crawl into a hole and remain out of sight for the rest of your life. Temptation will always be there, but you can accept these thoughts as normal and use them to remind you of all the reasons why you really do love your guy.

> People only see what they are prepared to see.
>
> RALPH WALDO EMERSON

Real Confessions

Are you still convinced that other women out there never compare their favorite guy to other men around them? Well, they do. Remember, no matter how bizarre your thoughts may seem, you're not alone. Women everywhere admit that they dare to compare, but they learn how to keep these assessments from ruining their relationship. Here are some examples.

- "I hear my friends bragging about their fabulous boyfriends and I make things up about mine just because I want everyone to think we have the perfect relationship. Then, I remind myself that maybe these other women are making up a few things too. Nobody's relationship is perfect."—*Lynette, age 35*

- "I see these guys out at night and they wear funky shirts that make them look cool. So what do I do? I go out and buy the same shirts for my boyfriend and threaten to disown him if he doesn't put them on. But then he does something really sweet and it reminds me that he doesn't need a funky shirt to be a great guy."—*Michelle, age 26*

- "More than once, I've daydreamed about this guy I work with. Sometimes I feel guilty and I'm terrified other people can tell what's going on in my head. The funny thing is, other women who've spent a lot of time with him can't stand him. Maybe he's appealing to me because I don't know him well."—*Jenna, age 24*

- "This woman I know always goes on and on about all the presents her boyfriend buys her and how she just knows he's the one for her. I seriously hate her for it. I know it's childish, but I don't even want to hang out with her because she makes me doubt my own relationship. I have to keep reminding myself that she's only bragging because she's insecure."—*Kate, age 32*

- "Sometimes when I'm annoyed with Steve, I doodle and end up pairing my name with other men's last names. I just try to see if an ex's name has a better ring to it than his does. Sometimes you just need to think about other guys to get your feelings straight about the one you're with. If the one you're with is right, these comparisons help you realize it."—*Mary Beth, age 29*

- "When Rob showed up at my office on Valentine's Day with balloons, I felt like I had won because he did something different.

The other women just received flowers. Now when I'm tempted to compare him in a negative way to another guy, I try to remember these great things he's done that make him better than other men."—*Ellie, age 32*

The Honest Conclusion

If you've answered these questions and determined that your wandering eye is a symptom of a larger problem in the relationship, you should be honest with yourself—and him—and end it. Easier said than done, of course, but if you find yourself nodding your head at these telltale points, realize that some part of you is already committed to leaving him. Breaking things off with a guy is painful even if you know he's not right for you. But the pain of a breakup is nothing compared to the torture of an unfulfilling long-term relationship. In case you need a little push to get you moving, consider these absurd alternatives.

> The Greek word for temptation means to test, to try, to prove.
>
> SELWYN HUGHES

Keep the Relationship Going

You can stay with your guy for years to come and become more and more complacent and intertwined, even though you know deep inside that he's not right for you. If you choose this option, you might go to parties and spend the evening checking out other men and being jealous of women who look like they're lucky in love. This can lead to feeling bitter and resentful because you are missing out on the life you were meant to live with a guy who would have made you happy. At some point you might even feel tempted to leave him for someone else, but you won't be able to do it very easily because you've already committed so much time and energy to the relationship. At that point, you will share the same friends, and perhaps even share the same house and kids. The longer you stay with a guy who isn't right for you, the more intertwined your lives will become and the harder it will be to leave him.

Search for a Band-Aid

You can also try to change him or yourself to make the relationship work, but this option isn't very appealing obviously. People rarely change and when they do, the changes often don't last. Sometimes people get married and have kids thinking these experiences will bring them closer together and help the relationship. But instead, they find that they only become more disenchanted and grow further apart when life gets more complicated.

For this option to work, you will probably need to go to counseling together before you even consider engagement. But why would you want to do such a thing when you can call it off and meet that special person out there who fits with you naturally? It makes more sense to break up and wait for the right person, than it does to try to make the wrong one fit.

Act Now

If you have only lukewarm feelings for your guy and you know your relationship is lacking, it's time to end it. You have to be able to make a commitment to him, and you can't do that if you are yearning for something (or someone) else. If you are comparing him to other guys regularly, and you wish you were with them or wish he would change, you clearly can't make that commitment.

So as hard as it is to call it quits, you must break it off. Don't wait until Valentine's Day is over. Don't wait until his birthday has passed or until you attend your friend's wedding because he's your date. There is never a right time to break up with a guy. Instead, hold your breath and dive in knowing that you're doing what's right for you and for him.

Positive Comparisons

Men are like little snowflakes, each with their own unique designs and jagged edges. They can melt quickly away or cling to any available surface. They can be big or small, cute, or sort of dirty looking. Each is dainty and pretty in its own way. Go ahead, call your boyfriend "dainty and pretty" and see what kind of reaction you get.

The point is that your boyfriend definitely does have unique things about him that make you love him. Perhaps he's not the hottest man alive, but he has a special mischievous smile he flashes whenever he's doing something to annoy you. He might not be as rich as Bill Gates, but he works hard and buys you cute, meaningful gifts. When pitted against another guy in the comparison game, there are areas in which your boyfriend will win every time. Focus on these positive comparisons. Identify those unique things about him that make him more special to you than any other man on earth.

Remember, being in a committed relationship doesn't mean you're cut off from the rest of the world. Don't forget that even though you are the most beautiful, charming, and perfect woman ever, it's inevitable that your boyfriend will find other women attractive in the same way you find other men attractive. It's important that you're both honest with each other about what you need and want out of your relationship. If you feel like you don't get enough affection or he feels like you don't spend enough time with him, you should both be comfortable sharing these feelings with each other. Over the years, you'll both change and you'll both have different needs. If you aren't open with each other about these needs, you'll feel like you need to turn elsewhere for fulfillment.

Regardless of how good your relationship is, every now and then you will still notice the hot celebrity on television or sneak a peek at a cute guy in line at the grocery store and think, "Wow, now he's better looking than my guy." But the thought will be fleeting and it might even make you laugh by the hundredth time you do it. Because now you know the truth: wherever you look, you can find a guy who has one up on your boyfriend somehow. On this planet of over 6 billion people, there will always be a guy who is cuter, smarter, better dressed, or richer than the one you're with. The answer to the question "Is there someone better out there?" will always be yes. So maybe that's not a question we should be asking at all.

chapter three

The Real Thing, Baby

Regardless of how your relationship started, the beginning or "honeymoon period" is similar for all couples in many ways. You're both on your best behavior, you feel like the other person is *so* right for you, and neither of you can imagine life being much better. During this time, you can talk for five hours straight and wonder where the time went. If you decide you need ice cream at 2 A.M., he gets dressed and cheerfully drives to the grocery store to grab you a pint. He even plays a cheesy love song in the car on the way and thinks about how adorable you are with no makeup on. If he gets stuck at work and can't pick you up, you don't mind. You think it's cute that he's important and busy. You can spend an entire week together and still feel like you haven't had enough of each other. Life is simply grand.

But no matter how good your relationship is, the newness inevitably wears off. It might take two months, six months, or over a year for this change to occur, but it will, and this isn't necessarily a bad thing. Transitioning into a new phase means that both of you get to experience "the real thing," —the reality of what life together is truly like. During this time, you may find yourself questioning whether or not he's right for you like you never have before. All the things you adored about him will seem a little less heavenly than they once did, and you'll try to remember why you started dating him in the first place. You'll ponder whether or not this "real thing" is the *right* thing.

> An object in possession seldom retains
> the same charm that it had in pursuit.
>
> PLINY THE YOUNGER

Is the Honeymoon Over?

You might be asking, "How can the honeymoon period be over so soon? Isn't it supposed to last a few years? How can he be right if he's driving me crazy after three months?" Well, the truth is that he might *not* be the right guy for you, and the things that happen during this time period can be signs of an early demise. But they might also be par for the course, typical changes that will eventually make your relationship stronger. When the idyllic moments seem a thing of the past, take a step back and look at how your relationship has changed. If you look honestly at your relationship, then you will find signs that will help you decide whether or not to move forward.

The Strange Changes

While you can expect some changes in your relationship, they shouldn't be so bad that they worry you or make you want to flee. It's more like when soft, gooey cookie dough becomes firm and brown in the oven. The more familiar association still tastes good, but it's not quite so fresh and mushy. If the changes are more significant, they are indicative that a bigger problem is at hand. Use this checklist to determine if the more "real" relationship you now have is one you should be getting out of.

Little Habits
You never noticed his little habits before, and now they are annoying you almost daily. He clips his toenails in the bathroom with the door open and it drives you nuts. He accuses you of building a fort around the sink with all of your bottles of beauty ointments, one he knocks over every time he tries to wash his hands. But he watches television on mute with subtitles. What's up with that? You're certain you don't do anything quite so irritating.

We all have little habits and his will start to bug you. This change is quite typical and not cause for alarm. You should be concerned only if:

- He has a little drug *habit* he failed to tell you about until now.
- He has the *habit* of calling you nasty names like "wench" and "tramp."
- He *habitually* "forgets" to show up for dates.
- He has gotten into the *habit* of coming over only when he's drunk.

Minor Squabbles

It used to be pretty clear that whoever owned the car would drive. Now he holds on to the sides of his seat with a death grip every time you step on the gas. Eventually he refuses to let you behind the wheel because he just doesn't trust "women drivers." You're not quite so fond of his driving either. After all, he's the one with the traffic violations on his license. Little disagreements will occur for the first time once the luster wears off, and despite all the sarcastic remarks you both utter under your breath, they are no big deal. You should be concerned about them only if:

- He screams and yells at you during these squabbles or threatens you in any way.
- The disagreements become regular parts of your interaction every time you're together.
- You're disagreeing about things that are fundamentally important to you, like religious beliefs or personal values.
- It takes days to make up after the smallest little argument.

Less Patience

You used to spend forever getting ready to go out on a date and he would wait patiently while reading your IKEA catalog. Now he's, well, a little more harried. In fact, last week he came upstairs, unplugged your hair dryer midblow, and yelled, "Are you going to take all night?" He just doesn't have the patience he used to have, but you're not a fan of his "Just give me two more minutes until they show the score" line either.

When two people spend a lot of time together, they always have moments when they feel a little irritated with each other.

They eventually find a way to let off steam without getting angry every time. A change in behavior is not a big deal unless:

- It's a drastic 180 and you don't have any idea who he is anymore.
- You feel like you have to jump whenever he asks for something because he'll get angry if you don't.
- He seems hell-bent on changing you to be the way he wants you to be.
- He's so "comfortable" that he couldn't care less what you think of the way he behaves. He says things like, "If you don't like it, leave."

Nothing endures but change.

HERACLITUS

A New Level of Honesty

Honesty is great in a relationship, right? So it's good news when the two of you open up the floor and say what's on your mind. You nix the hair gel and he tosses out a few "no ways" when you put on your new glittery tube top. You take it upon yourself to inform him that white socks are a huge faux pas with almost every pants/shoe combo on the planet. Likewise, he tells you he never liked your ditsy friends from work and he doesn't want to have dinner with them again . . . ever. The two of you share a new level of open, honest communication. It is a good thing when you feel like you can express your opinions to one another. This change is a problem only if:

- He's so honest that he's insulting. He says things like, "Your makeup is so caked on it makes you look like a mime. Too bad you're not quiet like one."
- When he decides to "tell all," you find out he was lying about something major like a criminal record, a child from a previous relationship, or his age.
- When you try to have an open, honest conversation with him, he doesn't receive it well. He yells at you when you tell him your feelings or things that are bothering you.
- You sense that the honesty isn't "real" honesty after all. In other words, he swears he's never been with another woman and that he owns a million-dollar summer home and you know he's full of crap.

Diverted Attention

He never wanted to go out with the guys before and now it seems like every weekend one night is reserved for these beer hogs, some of whom you've never even met. You don't hang out with your friends very often, so why is he doing it? You both start spending a little time apart here and there even when you're in the same room. You talk to him when he's watching television and he grunts an answer. Three weeks later he swears he never agreed to go see the community theater group perform *Little Red Riding Hood*. You have more time to talk about day-to-day things because you see each other more often, but there's one little problem—you don't always pay attention to what the other person is saying.

It's natural and healthy for both of you to start living your own lives again once you get past the initial fascination with one another. When the excitement wears off, you'll start to care more about the things you always cared about when you were on your own—your own friends, your activities, and your interests. This change is a problem only if:

- His attention is diverted so far that he's now seeing a couple of other girls on the side.
- You feel like he's never listening to you, doesn't care what you're saying, and hopes that you'll just shut up.
- You don't feel like paying attention to him—at all—because you just don't like him anymore.
- The relationship is lopsided—one of you is doing all the listening and caring, and the other just tunes out.

Sharing Responsibility

When the two of you first met, he paid for everything. He would insist that you put your wallet away. At home, you would pour him drinks and bring him the remote control. But one night, everything changed. He accepted that $20 bill you offered at dinner and that was *more* than half the price! And then you decided to let him get his own darn drink for a change. After all, you're not a waitress.

It's normal to begin to share responsibility for dates, payments, and activities at some point in the relationship. When the courting phase is over and you're both confident that you have won the affection of the other person, of course you're going to cut down on that "I'm so sweet and polite that I'll do everything" routine. This change is an issue only if:

- One person's definition of "sharing" is making the other person pick the restaurant or foot the bill all the time.

- "Sharing" becomes a tit-for-tat game. At dinner he pulls out a calculator to tell you how much you owe and he reminds you that it's your turn to treat.
- He expects you to share your cash, credit cards, and cosign for his $5,000 loan.
- He wants you to be open to sharing him with another girl.

I think that men know how to romance a woman and most do it well, at least for a time, otherwise women wouldn't marry them. The problem is that most of them begin to rest on their laurels.

NICHOLAS SPARKS

You're Not Alone

Are you still unconvinced this type of change in a relationship is typical? Do you believe that if you just met the right guy, the honeymoon period would never end, that he would continue to clean his apartment before you visit and jump up ten minutes early in the morning just to brew your coffee? Guess again. No guy is perfect. You might find a man who will brew your coffee in the morning but refuses to clean up after himself, or one who listens to what you say even when he's watching a game but forgets your anniversary. You have to decide what you need and what you can live without, because every guy has his faults and little annoying quirks. In fact, real women in extremely happy, committed relationships have confirmed this fact. They remember with great clarity those moments when their own relationship began to become a little less picture perfect. Here's what some of them had to say:

- "At first he would always show up wearing an ironed dress shirt, his face cleanly shaven. Then I noticed he stopped shaving. A few weeks after that, he started wearing T-shirts. Now I have to beg him to get dressed up when we go out with friends."—*Marissa, age 28*

- "The first six months we were dating, he would say, 'You look good in anything you wear.' Now he doesn't hesitate to tell me how he really feels. He offers his opinion on my outfits even when I don't ask."—*Carrie, age 34*

- "He used to act like he loved talking to my mother because he was trying to impress me. He would chat with her on the phone and ask her about her day. Now, when she calls, I have to put my hand over the receiver and beg him to say 'hi' to her."—*Christine, age 30*

- "In the beginning, he always had a restaurant picked out, and this elaborate plan for after dinner. Now he says 'Uh, what do you wanna do tonight?' and if I don't answer, he just keeps watching TV."—*Katie, age 29*

- "At first he sent me bouquets of flowers at work. In fact, I thought he was going overboard with the whole gift thing. Then, he stopped sending bouquets and started sending cards instead. These days, if I drop enough hints, he *might* buy me flowers at the supermarket."—*Sharon, age 40*

- "I distinctly remember that he used to have trouble actually sleeping when he stayed at my apartment. He was so excited to see me that he wouldn't go to bed until I fell asleep. Now I couldn't drag him out of bed if there was a fire."—*Jen, age 37 relationship retrograde* We're not always thrilled with the little changes that occur in a relationship, but these changes are a normal part of getting to know someone. So when your guy is driving you nuts, remind yourself that all guys go through this transformation and it doesn't mean you've picked a loser. Here are a few typical changes:

BEFORE He slept in brand-new boxers and showered thoroughly before crawling into bed.
NOW He plays basketball, does a "quick rinse-off," and sleeps naked except for sweaty socks.

BEFORE You fell for an adorable guy with a cute smile.
NOW After staring at his face up close for months and months, you finally notice that his cleft chin makes his face look like a heinie.

BEFORE You couldn't eat for weeks because he made you so nervous.
NOW Your appetite is back and you defend your cookies with a vengeance when he tries to snag one.

BEFORE You thought his favorite ripped T-shirt made him look cuter.

NOW You buy him several new T-shirts and the ripped one mysteriously disappears.

BEFORE You offered to go just about anywhere with him as long as it made him happy.

NOW You threaten to break up with him if he makes you hang out one more time in the dingy pub near his apartment.

BEFORE When you started sleeping over at his place, his bathroom was spotless, his dishes were clean, and his living room floor was vacuumed.

NOW He's through with his obligatory apartment cleaning. His kitchen is covered with crusty nacho bits and you have to wear hip boots when you use his bathroom.

BEFORE His friends seemed well behaved and they asked you intelligent questions about your life.

NOW His friends speak in curse words and ask you if you know any hot girls they can bang.

Sizing Up the Switch

You know you've left the honeymoon phase far behind when that solitary rose on your doorstep becomes a thing of the past and in its place sit your boyfriend's muddy sneakers that he wants you to throw into the laundry. For a while you might feel like you're not even dating the same guy anymore because his habits, behavior, and even his look have gotten a little more au naturel. But it's not all bad—this change can be nice in some ways. It means you can relax a little, shave your legs less often, and allow him to see pictures of those weird cousins you were worried would scare him off. But if he's not the right guy for you, you'll find some of the changes in the relationship downright disturbing. So before you completely accept your new, more true-to-life boyfriend, ask yourself a couple of questions.

Any change, even a change for the better, is always accompanied by drawbacks and discomforts.

ARNOLD BENNETT

Do You Ever Feel the Urge to Run Away?

It's one thing to be angry when you stumble upon his porn collection; it's another thing to be scarred for life. Each of us has our own deal breakers. You might feel like you cannot live with pets under any circumstances. Someone else might think meeting a dog lover is like finding a kindred spirit. Set your limits and stick to them. Regardless of how harmless his behavior may be, if you know you can't spend the rest of your life dealing with it, there's no use prolonging your pain. Do yourself and him a favor and end things now.

Look out for other more definitive changes in his behavior and attitude, changes that are not acceptable under any circumstances. Break things off if:

- He gets verbally or physically abusive.
- He tries to manipulate or control you by telling you what to wear and keeping you from hanging out with your friends.
- He becomes unbearably needy, asking you every five minutes if you care about him and chastising you for not spending enough time with him.
- He no longer cares about the relationship unless you're giving him money or sex.
- He's unemployed and living on your couch with no plans to find a new job.
- He's doing drugs or drinking excessively.
- He stops calling you and stops planning dates. You feel like you're making all the effort.

Some of the most dangerous men can be so sweet in the first few months of a relationship. This is their mode of operation. Once they know you're interested in them, they begin showing their true colors, and those true colors are downright frightening. The changes you experience might annoy you but they should not make you feel anxious and fearful or hurt and unloved. If they do, you need to call it quits today.

Are Your Expectations Realistic?

If you decide that you do want to break up with your guy because you cannot handle the way he's changed, just make sure your expectations are realistic. Remember that plenty of his habits and behaviors that emerge as you get more comfortable are just typical guy gunk. They might not be pleasant. In fact, they might drive you absolutely crazy sometimes, but that doesn't mean he's not a good boyfriend and you don't have a good relationship. As long as you're dating a heterosexual male, you can expect to go a little bit crazy sometimes. Keep in mind that we do a few things that drive guys nuts too (but just a few). The differences between the sexes keep all relationships full of fabulous friction.

Typical Guy Gunk

Guys don't like to be lumped into one category any more than women do, but there are certain qualities and habits that they just can't deny are typical of their gender. There will always be exceptions to the rule, but let's just assume for a minute that your guy is not an exception. You can expect a few things:

- He will not give you his undivided attention if you talk to him when he's watching sports or his favorite television programs.
- He will forget once in a while that he promised you he'd go with you to Home Depot and he'll schedule a basketball game for the same night.

- He will get complacent and stop doing the little things so often (flowers, cute notes, etc.).
- He will buy your gift the day of your birthday, or if you're lucky, the day before. If you beg him to buy his mother's birthday gift early, he will look very confused and then ask you why you're stressed about it.
- He will not understand why a bathtub needs to be cleaned more than once every six months.
- He will stop offering his help, opinion, and advice when you need it (picking restaurants, deciding what to do on a Saturday, etc.) and start offering it when you don't need it (how you should be driving, what type of TV you should buy).
- He will not read the "How to Improve Our Relationship" book you leave on his pillow (or in his briefcase, or duct taped to the television remote).

Our Cute Little Quirks

Just as men have their typical behaviors, we, too, have our cute little quirks, though guys don't always find them so cute. Remember that he's learning to live with a more natural you as well so cut him some slack. Here's what real men say are their biggest peeves with women:

- "When my dog sheds it doesn't bother me, but it really makes me sort of queasy when I find her long strands of hair on the bathroom floor."—*Matt, age 28*
- "If I tell her our reservation is for eight o'clock, she thinks that means that we need to leave the house at eight."—*Jeremy, age 31*

- "She doesn't tell me when something's wrong and then gets mad at me because I don't know. I'm not psychic."—*Tony, age 36*
- "She wears socks to bed even if it's one hundred degrees out. I feel like they radiate heat under the covers."—*Dave, age 27*
- "She'll ask me a hundred times which type of cheese she should get at the grocery store and then when I tell her, she ends up getting the one she wants anyway."—*Mike, age 30*
- "She's always asking the waiter if they have a low-cal option. I just don't understand why she can't appreciate chicken wings."—*Drew, age 23*
- "She talks and talks. Then, in all seriousness, she talks more. She talks when we're getting ready to go somewhere. She talks in the car. She talks during every lull in the movie. I am truly astounded sometimes at a woman's need to verbalize."—*Mark, age 29*

Delightful Discoveries

Though you will reveal more of your gritty side when you're comfortable in the relationship, you should discover new things you like about each other too. The relationship isn't all downhill after the honeymoon period. Sure you notice that he's not quite so charming when he's playing beer pong, but you like the fact that he loves to hang out with a big group of friends. And yes, you see that he's not quite as cute when his hair is all matted down in the morning, but you are glad he just doesn't care what he looks like sometimes. The little quirks and annoyances are balanced out by all the good things you're learning about each other. The relationship hasn't deteriorated; it's just changed into a friendship with romantic moments that are more real and intimate. Now you can both be yourselves and enjoy the genuine connection that you have.

If you don't make any positive discoveries as you get to know a guy, that's not a good sign. So think about your relationship. Did he just get worse once you got to know him or did you also start to see new, cute, lovable things that you didn't notice at first? Your great finds can be anything. They can be things that everyone adores or things that are special just to you. Think about what you learned about your guy as you got to know him.

Unfounded Fears

Perhaps you discovered that your fears about him were unfounded and that he was different than you first imagined he would be. For instance, maybe he came off as lazy and now you know that he works hard but just doesn't like to talk about his job. Or perhaps you were afraid he wouldn't be romantic, but now you realize that he is but he shows it in weird ways like leaving love notes taped under the toilet seat. Of course, you also have new fears—you never knew he liked skydiving and now you fear for his life. But you're also pleasantly surprised by how wrong your first impression was in some ways.

Shared Interests

Maybe you're discovering that the two of you have fun doing the same types of activities. For example, you love amusement parks for the games but you're scared to death of the rides. You never thought you would meet another person who felt the same way, but he agrees with you. Perhaps you find that you both think Italian food is fantastic and action adventure movies are the best. In sharing your real feelings and preferences, you discover new ways in which you're similar.

> In a great romance, each person plays
> a part the other really likes.
>
> ELIZABETH ASHLEY

Similar Energy Level

There are some commonalities you really can't identify until you've been together for at least a few months. For example, how long do you like to play tennis before you need a nap? Do you prefer to walk or drive? After a while, when you get into a rhythm together, you realize that you have very similar energy levels . . . or you don't. You might find out that he loves to sleep late every day just like you do. You won't be similar in every way, but you should be making some discoveries that are bringing you closer together, not further apart.

What If There Was No Honeymoon Period?

If this entire chapter seems a little bizarre to you—you can't think of when your relationship started to change, and you don't remember any lovey-dovey moments—it could be because your relationship didn't have a honeymoon period. If you never experienced any initial excitement when you started dating your guy, this might be a sign of an underlying problem. Two people are never on their best behavior again like they are at the beginning of a relationship. If you weren't trying to make the relationship work back then, you probably never will. Even if you knew each other before you started dating, when romance came into the picture, things should have gotten a little dreamy. Do you remember a time that was really special, one full of fun and excitement? If you don't, maybe you didn't start off on a very good note and you need to explore why.

The Initial Glue

What was the initial glue that made your relationship stick? His looks? Sex appeal? Sense of humor? Many women say a combination of factors made them go out with their guy more than once. Some women can't pinpoint what they liked about him but they knew they wanted to get to know him better. What brought you and your guy together? If you think the initial glue that stuck you together wasn't strong enough, break it off. Some of the wrong reasons to start a relationship include:

- A SELF-ESTEEM BOOST. You were feeling kind of insecure and really wanted a person to dote on you and lift you out of the doldrums. This guy showered you with attention and made you feel loved. Now that you're feeling more confident, you're not so sure he's the right fit for you.

- GLITZ AND GLAMOUR. He has an apartment in New York, one in London, and a beach house in Malibu. He knows lots of important people and gets you into exclusive clubs. Now that you've explored the life of the jet-setters, you're sort of over it. But you're finding that glitz and glam is all he really has to offer, and that's not enough for you.

- A PLACE TO LIVE. You just moved to a new city and you desperately need a place to stay. You go on a few dates and he offers to let you move in with him. When you finally have enough money to move, you feel torn because you like him but you don't love him for anything other than his apartment.

- A FILLER GUY. You hadn't dated in a while and he came along. You were so tired of being the single one and it just seemed like the answer to all of your problems. You could envision the two of you hanging out on holidays and you were excited just to have someone to cuddle with on weekends. Now that things have gotten a little more comfortable, you realize that having just any old guy there is not enough to make you happy.

- A CAREER BOOST. He worked at your dream company so you decided to go out with him. He got you a job there, but you've since discovered that you're not enamored with him. You feel weird about breaking it off because you don't want to seem ungrateful, but you don't want to keep dating him out of obligation.

- HE LOOKED GOOD ON PAPER. He had all of those qualities that should have, in theory, made him a good match. He was cute, smart, had an M.B.A., a great job, and was taller than you when you wore heels. In other words, he had a stellar "guy resume." But now that you're getting to know the real him, you realize that you never did like his personality. All those credentials just aren't enough to make you want to stick around.

Mutual Indifference

Have you ever heard the phrase "proximity is intimacy"? If you're both living in the same apartment building or neighborhood, and you see each other on occasion on the street or at the laundromat, at some point you might decide to get together romantically. But beware of getting involved in a relationship that is born of convenience. He's your hookup buddy. He's your "friend with benefits." You love spending time with him, curling up next to him, and bringing him as your safety date to formal events, but he's just not "it." You might get so used to hanging out with him that you forget that you weren't really committed to each other to begin with. If you're dating a guy because he's close by but you feel ambivalent toward him, break it off. Don't waste your time dating someone who is clearly not right for you.

We waste time looking for the perfect lover,
instead of creating the perfect love.

TOM ROBBINS

The Telltale Takeoff

Your relationship might have bypassed the honeymoon stage because the guy wasn't on his best behavior in the beginning or he just wasn't into the relationship. If you think that might be the reason why you don't remember a honeymoon period (i.e., you were too nervous or anxious about what his next move would be), you have a problem on your hands. A guy's behavior in the first few months sets the stage for the years to come. If he doesn't treat you well when you're new in his life, you can only expect things to get worse when he lets his guard down. If you feel like the relationship isn't working now and you're not getting what you need from him, examine the beginning again. If he wasn't great to you then, maybe he's the one who is in it for the wrong reasons. When a guy's heart is into making the relationship work, a few blatant signs should be present. Look for them.

Impeccable Manners

If he really cares about you, when he first meets you, he shows up at your place early for a date, looking like he just stepped out of a Polo advertisement. He says "please" and "thank you," opens the door for you, and insists on paying the bill even when you make a half-hearted lunge for your wallet.

Great Hygiene

Even if he's normally a dirty pig, when he first meets you, if he likes you, he cleans up his act. A guy in love is mortified if he has a little piece of lettuce in his teeth when he's having dinner with a girl he likes. If his teeth contain a big chunk of lettuce, some tuna fish, and a little morsel of something you can't identify, he isn't showing you respect.

Genuine Adoration

Did he treat you with kindness and consideration? Did he call you "beautiful" or "adorable" or at least appear to be thinking these things? If he didn't treat you well when he thought you were absolutely perfect, he's not going to do it after he gets to know your quirks and flaws.

Putting You First

When he started dating you, he should have put your interests first. His friends, sports, or video games should not have been above you in the pecking order. He should have been thrilled to have the opportunity to spend time with you. The day always comes when a guy refuses to miss a big game to take you to dinner, but he shouldn't be this much of a meathead from the start.

Making Plans

In the first few months of the relationship, your guy should have been making grandiose plans for the two of you together. He should have been talking about daytrips you could take or vacation destinations. Of course, this dreamy talk does decline over time, but it shouldn't be completely absent from the beginning.

No Excuses

While he might do plenty of annoying and careless things now that you know him well, in the beginning, he should have been making every effort to call on time, show up on time, and remember your birthday. A guy is on his best behavior when he's trying to win your heart. If he's not on his best behavior, you have to assume he's just not interested in a real relationship.

The bottom line: if things are confusing in your relationship now, and you're not sure what you want, ask yourself if you were ever really happy. Did he treat you well at the beginning? Did you have any fun and exciting times? If you can't answer yes to these questions, you definitely need to end it today. As you each discover each other's faults and foibles, your heart has to be in the relationship to keep it going. You have to be committed enough to keep moving forward even if you aren't thrilled with everything you see all the time. If your heart was never fully in the relationship in the first place, and it's not now, it never will be.

chapter four

Conflicts of Interest

Nothing brings out raw ugliness in a couple like a good screaming match. Once you've had a couple of huge blowout fights, you may have a few reservations. You ask yourself, "Can we possibly love each other if we are fighting about something as trivial as what to have for dinner? Can we really recover from a six-hour yell-a-thon that wakes up the entire neighborhood?"

Take heart, because you're not alone in your worries—or your fighting. Couples everywhere are asking these same questions, and the answer, surprisingly, is yes, you can have a normal, happy relationship even after you've screamed, yelled, cried, slammed doors, and chucked open containers of food at each other. Why? There are plenty of theories, but they all come down to this: fighting itself is not the real problem. It's *how* you fight that makes or breaks a relationship.

Time and again, people who study conflict (and those of us who have lived through it) prove that a couple's attitude and behavior during a fight are much more telling than the fight itself. So if you think your fights are a large, blinking neon sign that you should call it quits with your guy, read on. You'll learn that even the happiest couples fight, but they survive because they fight constructively. They work together to resolve their conflicts and do what it takes to make their relationship stronger.

> It is better to debate a question without settling it than to settle a question without debating it.
>
> JOSEPH JOUBERT

Universal Truths

Believe it or not, experts have plenty of positive things to say about fighting. They say it's a sign a couple is communicating, sharing their feelings on big issues, and ironing out kinks in their relationship. Some even go so far as to say that couples who fight and argue are better off than those who keep their issues bottled up inside. Of course that doesn't mean fighting is fun, but with this "fighting is healthy" principle in mind, you can at least take a moment to feel good about your open, communicative relationship.

The truth is that constructive fighting can bring you and your guy closer together by giving you the opportunity to reach a new level of understanding. But what makes a fight constructive? What allows some couples to survive the strife and become even stronger while others break up? All couples fight about different things, in different ways, for different reasons, but those who are happy and stay together all have a few things in common:

- A routine way of fighting
- A desire to make up, forgive, and forget
- Positive interactions with each other that balance out the negative ones
- The willingness to accept that some issues between them will never be resolved

We'll explore each of these elements in this chapter.

Fight Nice

Most people assume that the strength of a relationship can be gauged easily by observing how often a couple fights and how intense their fights are. And this theory does make sense. Screaming and throwing things at each other certainly seem more destructive than just talking problems out over coffee. But experts who study fighting conclude that it doesn't matter how frequent or how intense your fights are. In fact, a couple that bickers constantly or yells loudly during their fights can be just as happy as a more diplomatic couple (barring physical or verbal abuse, addressed later in the chapter). What really makes a relationship survive is a feeling of goodwill that surfaces at some point during the argument or immediately afterward.

"Goodwill" means you both make an effort to acknowledge the other person's point of view and say something validating. For example, you get mad at him for showing up late all the time. At first, he resists and yells back, "I'm not late. You expect me to come over too early." But then he thinks about it, realizes he's being a jerk, and says, "I hear what you mean dearest sweet love. You are right. I should call if I'm hitting traffic on my way over." Now that sounds a little hokey and it might even seem far-fetched. Most of us make comments when we're angry that are anything but validating. But if you really think about your most recent fight, chances are you will recall some moment where one of you finally gave in and started to listen. It might have taken a few hours or even a few days, but eventually, someone reached out with the olive branch in hand.

In a good relationship, one person isn't giving in first all the time. Each person does it at some point. But regardless of who initiates the reconciliation, both people welcome it. You're committed to each other and you want to make the relationship work. You might have a moment or two during the fight when you think, "Actually, I don't want to make this work; I want him to go away," but when the fight is over, you realize that you would never want him to go away for good. If you or your guy have done any of the things that follow, you are on the right fighting track. So shake hands and congratulate each other on your superb squabbling skills.

- You've said things like "Okay, I understand what you're saying" or "I hear you. I'm sorry." (And you meant it! Sarcasm doesn't count.)

- You've said something playful or silly to lighten the mood, like "I know you are but what am I?"
- You've made physical gestures that indicate remorse or a connection, like hugging, touching an arm, or even a playful pinch.
- You've smiled at one another, winked, or made another facial expression that indicated an attempt to stop the argument.
- You've used gestures or words that demonstrate a commitment to the relationship, like "I love you and I don't want to fight" or "The dog hates when we argue."
- You went from being angry (yelling, stomping, etc.) to feeling sad (crying, moping, etc.).

The art of love is largely the art of persistence.

ALBERT ELLIS

A Familiar Groove

You've learned by now that if you want your relationship to work, you will inevitably have to get used to each other's personalities, quirks, and habits. Likewise, you'll also have to adapt to each other's fighting style. If he's a yeller and you're not, he's probably going to scare you to death when you have an argument. But if you're both yellers, or you're simply used to yelling because your mother dealt with her stress that way, his fighting style might not bother you at all. A happy couple has a "fighting groove," a way of interacting when they are mad that they are both used to. Some signs that you've found your groove include:

- You're both short tempered and you get riled up when you fight. Someone else might think this type of behavior is too harsh, but since you both do it, it doesn't bother either of you.

- Neither of you can stand bickering, so you ignore each other until someone gives in and talks. People keep telling you that ignoring one another is counterproductive, but because you both like this approach, it works for you.

- He refuses to look at you when you yell at him, but you've learned that if you put your eyeballs right up to his while you're telling him how you feel, he cracks a smile. By familiarizing yourself with his style, you've learned how to lighten up your arguments.

- You always fight when you're in the car because he's a nervous driver. You pretty much know he's going to start flipping out the minute you put your seat belt on. Because these fights are a pattern, you've learned how to prepare for them. You have maps handy and you tell him when to change lanes so he doesn't get so stressed out.

- You cry incessantly when the two of you argue. He used to feel like your tears were a sign of his own inadequacy, but now he realizes that crying is your natural response to stress. He's learned to pull you out of your sobbing spells by making funny faces.

Balancing Act

In a healthy, working relationship, the number of positive interactions a couple has should far outnumber the fights and tense moments. This is what experts refer to as a balanced relationship. So if you're arguing all the time and there's never any happy moment or warm connection between the two of you, you have a problem on your hands. Think about the time you spend with your guy. Is the situation always tense? Are you usually annoyed or angry? Is he always upset about something? Do you end up arguing at some point every time you're together? Most importantly, do you have happy times too and feel like you're emotionally connected? The balance in your relationship is out of whack if:

- You argue every time you see each other.
- Even when you're not arguing, you're mean to each other or aloof.
- Your fights are extremely intense, and you aren't very loving to each other when you make up. Intense fights should be followed by intense moments of reconciliation.
- You never feel any moments of true connection where you laugh together, hug each other, or validate one another in some other way.
- You notice that when you're with other people, you feel more relaxed because there's no conflict.
- You're exhausted every day from arguing and talking out the issues.

Common Sense

Some couples fight in a destructive manner. They have a knack for turning the smallest disagreement into a lifelong vendetta. Their arguments and battles take a toll on the relationship and eventually drive it into the ground. It's not because their fights are louder or last longer than everyone else's. It's because of the way they fight. Dr. John Gottman, an expert in marital stability and divorce prediction has identified four warning signs that occur during fighting. He calls these signs "The Four Horsemen of the Apocalypse." They are:

1. **Criticizing:** You attack each other's personality or character instead of the incident or specific issue that bugs you.

Example: You're mad at him for telling his brother about your speeding ticket. Instead of explaining to him that you prefer he keep these things between the two of you, you call him a big mouth and yell, "I can't trust you with anything." You're angry, so you dig right in and try to make him feel like a big loser. Then he criticizes you back, and calls you a typical woman driver.

2. **Contempt:** You enter into the fight with the intention of insulting and abusing your partner.

Example: He wants to control you so he tries to destroy your confidence with nasty insults. You feel like he's a wrecking ball, knocking you over every time he unleashes his anger.

3. **Defensiveness:** You deny the other person's accusations and make excuses for your behavior.

Example: He asks you not to make fun of his job. You keep doing it. He asks you again to give it a rest. You tell him he's too sensitive and that you have a right to make fun of him because he teases you all the time.

4. **Stonewalling:** One or both of you stops reacting, becomes silent, and ignores the other person. Communication ceases altogether.

Example: When you're fighting, he turns up the volume on the TV and refuses to respond. For the rest of the night, he acts like you aren't there. When you do finally communicate again, he pretends the argument didn't happen. When you try to bring up the issue that's bothering you, he starts ignoring you again.

Okay, after reading this list you're probably convinced that your relationship is doomed and you'll never have another healthy relationship for the rest of your life. But don't give up just yet.

Even in the best relationships, when our tempers are pushed to the max, sometimes we can't help but criticize our boyfriends with phrases like "All you care about is yourself." And what woman hasn't, at some point, set out to be a tad bit insulting just out of spite by yelling things like "Well at least I don't have a spare-tire stomach like you do." And who among us can claim they have never gotten defensive during an argument or given their guy the silent treatment? So if we take this list of bad behaviors to heart, we can pretty much assume that we're doomed to a life of solitude because we don't know how to fight constructively. But it's important to temper research findings with common sense.

Obviously none of us are angels and we are going to do things to each other that are not nice when we're arguing. Your relationship is not doomed simply because you do something mean to each other once in a while. But if these destructive behaviors make up the bulk of your daily communication, your relationship cannot survive, and quite frankly, why would you want it to?

to each his own Every couple has their own unique way of fighting and making up. What's important is that during each fight, you make an effort to reconcile and find a way to make the relationship work.

Here's what real women have to say about how they fight and why it works:

- "My husband and I yell at each other so loudly that our dog cowers under the coffee table. But both of us grew up in Italian homes with very expressive siblings and parents, so we're used to the energy level being high. Other people might think we're crazy, but we don't see our fights as a problem."—*Maria, age 44*

- "My ex and I almost never fought but we did have one big argument after I found out he was cheating on me. That one ended our relationship. Now I fight with my husband all the time about little things and even get into some pretty heated debates, but in the end, we both know the other person cares and we would never do anything to jeopardize what we have."—*Andrea, age 36*

- "I completely admit that I'm a nut job sometimes. I've thrown shoes, food, and even full glasses of soda at him during arguments. I've bit him and called him vicious names I can't repeat here. But we always make it through our arguments. Sometimes when I launch into my drama queen routine, he claps and says, 'Bravo!' and we both start laughing."—*Jenna, age 33*

- "My mom would always chew my dad out about something and he would wave his hand at her like he was trying to swat a bug. Then they would both shout obscenities at each other. But once it was over, they would act like nothing ever happened. They both just forgot about their fights and moved on. And they were happily married for fifty years."—*Anne, age 46*

- "He loves to give me the silent treatment. If I make him mad, he'll leave and come back hours later. Then he'll say to me, 'Are you over your little tantrum?' and we'll laugh and talk it out."—*Brooke, age 26*

- "Kevin used to get mad at me for bringing up a hundred problems at once. He would say, 'You keep a mental checklist of what I do wrong and then spring it on me.' I told him if he doesn't like it, I'll get him a walkie-talkie so he can hear about my peeves as they come up. He hasn't complained about my checklist since."—*Heather, age 34*

The Heart of the Matter

Once you've taken a good look at *how* you fight, take some time to think about *why* you fight. Research reveals that couples fight about the same issues for years and years, and most of the time, they never reach an agreement. So if you're arguing about money today, twenty years from now, you and your guy will probably still be arguing about money. Encouraging, right? But it's very normal for even happy couples to fight about the same issues time and again without ever actually reaching a resolution. So ask yourself, if your major issues with your guy are never resolved—for the rest of your life—are you okay with that? Before you answer this question, make sure you know what your major issues really are.

> I have never in my life learned anything from any man who agreed with me.
>
> DUDLEY FIELD MALONE

Typical Little Problems

Every couple has arguments over little things—what channel to watch, who left the light on all night in the bathroom, or who is going to take the dog for a walk when it's freezing outside. Plenty of these little tiffs escalate into bigger fights if they occur when one or both people are stressed out, overtired, or in a bad mood. Regardless of whom you're dating, you'll have these types of fights. They are inevitable problems all couples deal with, so don't doubt your relationship if these silly issues keep coming up.

They include things like:

Bad Timing

There will probably be times when he thinks he's being cute and you think he's being an ass. For example, you've had a bad day at work and you really need to tell him about it. He jokingly puts a piece of Scotch tape over your mouth when you're trying to talk to him. You freak out and yell at him for not listening to you, and the incident becomes a big discussion about why he's so insensitive to your work problems.

Un-Constructive Criticism

Sometimes he'll tell you something that's bugging him about you and couch it as "constructive criticism." For example, he tells you that you'd be more successful if you'd stop asking so many stupid questions when you talk to people. The truth is that he just didn't like the fact that you got along so well with his best friend and seemed so interested in his life. He felt jealous. So now he's finding something about you to nitpick. "Stupid questions?" you ask. "What is that supposed to mean?" The incident blossoms into a battle where he finally reveals what's really bothering him.

Meltdown Mode

You've been working late every night and you have a huge presentation tomorrow that you're frantically trying to finish. He shows up at your place, parks his butt on your couch, cracks open a beer, turns on the game, and turns up the

volume. Though you normally wouldn't mind his beer chug-
ging and game watching, in your hyper-stressed state, you are
completely annoyed that he's not focusing on you or giving
you a massage or jumping at your every whim to help you out
and calm you down a little bit. After all, if he was stressed
out, you would try to help him. As your anger boils over, you
decide that if you have to be miserable, he should be too! So
you go into total meltdown mode and you wipe that silly smile
off his face with a few choice words and a door slam.

Misinterpretations

He tells you he doesn't understand why you need three
pairs of black boots. From the tone of his voice, you think
that he's accusing you of being frivolous with your money.
You consider putting on the pair with the sharpest, highest
heel and kicking him in the groin. The incident blossoms into
a heated discussion about financial responsibility that ends
with you turning his jar of 10,000 pennies upside down on his
hardwood floor.

Eye Candy

He practically drools over women on the street and he
spends far too long in the bathroom with your Victoria's
Secret catalog. But you make one little comment about the hot
guy in the movie and he freaks out. He accuses you of flirting
with men and insists you're going to leave him for another guy.
But you remind him that he doesn't exactly keep his eyes to
himself. You end up in a big fight that ends with the two of
you admitting that you love each other and feel jealous when
the other person is attracted to someone else.

A Really "Guy" Thing to Do

He tells you that he's planning to come over Saturday night but calls halfway through the day to tell you he's going out with some friends instead. You get angry because he's standing you up at the last minute. He can't understand why you think it's the last minute, because he contacted you more than five hours in advance. You slam down the phone, he calls back, and the argument ensues.

Worst-Case Worries

You're feeling insecure because you have PMS. He calls you from a friend's house and you hear a girl's voice in the background. Who is she? Why is she there? Is that her giggling? What's so funny? Is he making faces behind your back? Is that why she's laughing? By the time you hang up, you're absolutely certain he's cheating on you. When he arrives at your place, you tell him off with tears streaming down your face. But he informs you that the girl was actually his friend's lesbian next-door neighbor.

More Serious Issues

While many arguments are typical, everyday tiffs, some are more serious. The serious ones may begin as something seemingly superficial, but underneath, a bigger issue is brewing. Your fight over who's taking out the trash might actually be about how you feel he's taking you for granted. That spat over what to do Saturday night might really be about how he feels you're not making enough of an effort with his friends. These bigger issues make you wonder whether or not he's really the guy for you. But remember—every couple has some big issues. Finding a new guy won't make every problem go away—he'll just come with a new set of problems that you have to learn to deal with. No relationship will ever be issue-free. You have to decide which issues you can live with and which ones are deal breakers for you.

Think about your fights and identify any larger problems lurking below the surface of your day-to-day arguments. If you sense there's more going on than just a surface issue, you'll need to make some firm decisions about your relationship.

On the Surface: You fight because he drinks all of your Snapple when he comes over but never replenishes the supply.
Real Issue: You think he's the human sponge, milking you for every penny he can get.

On the Surface: You fight because he's moving to a new neighborhood farther away and you don't want to drive there.
Real Issue: He's vague about where the relationship is going and his move makes you doubt his commitment even more.

On the Surface: You fight because you asked him not to smoke in your apartment and he did it anyway while you were out shopping.
Real Issue: He's not respecting your needs and wishes and this really ticks you off.

On the Surface: You get in a fight because he talks to his guy friends on the phone and then meets them out without considering your plans.

Real Issue: He isn't spending enough time with you, and you feel like he just doesn't care about you.

On the Surface: You fight because he comments that a woman on TV is hot.
Real Issue: He doesn't make you feel good about yourself, and he compares you to other women.

On the Surface: You fight because he wants to turn the air-conditioning on high and you're freezing.
Real Issue: You feel like he's selfish and always has to have his own way.

Remember, big issues often don't get resolved. In fact, experts have observed certain couples for decades and found that even though they are happy, they are still bickering over the same things. Take this discovery seriously. Repeat this sentence out loud: "I might end up fighting with him about the same things for the rest of my life." Can you live with that reality? You need to decide—do you still love him and still want to make it work even if none of your current problems are solved? Are the things you're fighting about deal breakers or can you live with them? This is an important question that you have to answer before you decide whether to keep him or let him go.

Turning Down the Volume

If you decide that the two of you have what it takes to make your relationship work despite your arguments, there are certain things you can do to tone down these stressful moments. Fighting takes a toll on your energy level and your peace of mind. It also eats away at time that you could use to enjoy each other and do fun things. So while you will have to accept the fact that fighting is a normal part of every relationship, you can also learn tools that will help you cut down on the amount of time you spend in a state of conflict.

> Peace is not the absence of conflict but the presence of creative alternatives for responding to conflict—alternatives to passive or aggressive responses, alternatives to violence.
>
> DOROTHY THOMPSON

Battle Lines

Every counselor, clergyman, shrink, and well-meaning best friend on the planet has tips on how to fight more constructively. You can attend seminars, watch videos, and find hundreds of books on the subject. You'll hear things like "Pick the right place and time to fight," "Don't roll your eyes. Watch your body language," and "Avoid personal attacks." But are these really practical tips for the real world? Chances are, when you're actually in the middle of a fight, these suggestions are the furthest thing from your mind. How easy life would be if we could really pick the time and place in which we fight (instead of yelling at each other on a street corner at noon) and avoid personal attacks (instead of pushing his buttons to drive him nuts).

Another favorite cliché solution is "Never go to bed angry." In theory, it would be nice if we could resolve our disagreements and still get eight hours of sleep. But what happens if you can't get the problem solved before bedtime? Are you supposed to stay up arguing until 6 A.M., then go to work an hour later? Despite this cliché, sometimes you can resolve the fight faster if you go to bed ticked off and wake up with a fresh perspective. If you find some of these "happy fight" suggestions a little ridiculous, you're not alone. The best way to fight more constructively is to learn by trial and error. Think about your conflicts when you're not actually in the middle of one and figure out what tactics work for you. Does your guy usually soften when you pick on him? Does he open up once you start listening? Think about the ways the two of you can move toward reconciliation once a fight begins and apply them the next time you start to bicker. Still struggling to figure out your fights and make them constructive? Here are a few tips:

Focus

You can make your fights more constructive by focusing on the issue at hand and not on everything else that bugs you about him (like his snoring or his filthy socks). Try to understand what he wants—does he just want to be left alone? Does he want to hear you say you love him? Does he want to feel like you appreciate him? And finally, *focus* on the fact that you love this person and want to make this relationship work. You're not very focused if you:

- Can't stop thinking, "I would love to slap him right now" while he's telling you something.

- Can't hear a word he's saying because you are yelling over him every time he tries to speak.
- Get madder and madder because you can't stop thinking about how he might commit the same offense again in the future.
- Can't resist the urge to bring up the annoying things he did last month even though they are irrelevant.
- Can't resist the urge to make fun of the way he dresses and tell him how dumb his jokes are just to make him feel insecure.

Connect

Two people connect when they send each other positive signals and communicate in subtle ways that they are on the same team. Even when you're arguing, you should be trying to connect with him and he should be trying to connect with you in some way. You might not really understand each other's point of view, but you can still make an effort to relate positively to him during an argument. A few ways to reach out include:

- Give him a gentle pinch to make him laugh.
- Say something outrageous like "No offense, but you remind me of Elton John."
- Draw a squiggly line on his arm with a magic marker.
- Try repeating back to him his accusations: "So I see that you think I'm a bitchy blob." He'll be happy you're listening and he might even laugh at how ridiculous his words actually sound.
- Pretend to call someone he hates and tell them all the things he says about them. When he freaks out, yell "Psych!" and cartwheel away.
- Pretend to call your mother and do the same.

pushing *buttons* No normal person enjoys fighting with someone they love. But we still do it and sometimes we go all out and push the other person's buttons out of spite. This type of reaction is not ideal, but it is normal. Here's what real women have to say about their ugliest moments during fights:

- "Sometimes I go right for his weakest spot—his salary. He feels like he doesn't make enough money. I really don't care how much money he makes but sometimes I act like I do just to bother him. I always feel sorry for making him feel bad."—*Samantha, age 27*

- "I'm a slammer. I slam doors and make a lot of noise. I've even ruined things of his, like one of his dry-clean-only shirts. I put it in the shower and turned the water on it. I'm not proud when I do things like this, but sometimes when you're angry, you just can't help it."—*Kristin, age 34*

- "One time when we were arguing, I took that little bucket thing out of the freezer and dumped all the ice over his head while he was watching TV. I really regret it because now, at least once a month, he dumps ice on me when I'm in the shower. I don't think he's ever going to let me forget it."—*Cindy, age 31*

- "My boyfriend is always struggling to stay in shape, so he's sensitive about his body. One time when we were fighting, I screamed, 'I don't want to date a fat guy anymore.' It was so mean. It took me weeks to convince him that I was only saying it to make him mad."—*Lori, age 26*

In all seriousness, anything you can do to communicate and connect will bring you closer together and help break down the walls you're putting up during arguments. Of course, he should be trying to do the same thing, but you might have to be the one to teach by example.

Let It Go

Keep in mind that a large part of getting along with someone is learning to relax when something is bothering you and deal with the issue maturely instead of letting it escalate into a fight. If you grew up with siblings, you've probably mastered this skill already. When you had a fight with a brother or sister, instead of getting angry, you'd put on a pair of headphones and turn up the music. That's mature, right? Okay, maybe it's not the best way to handle things, but after a while, you did learn that feeding into the fight was not always the best way to deal with the situation.

The same thing holds true for male-female relationships. Sometimes you just have to let his crap go. (Not literally. Don't drop his prized possessions out the window!) While you should never ignore destructive or abusive behavior, there are plenty of little things he will do that you can choose to overlook. You can just accept some of the things you don't like and avoid arguing altogether. Some of these things might include:

- He lets dishes pile up for two weeks before he puts them in the dishwasher. You can't expect him to do every little thing exactly the way you do it.

- He refuses to dance at weddings. There are things some men just feel stupid doing and often dancing is one of them.
- He offers suggestions and solutions when you just want to vent about a problem. All guys do it. Teaching him otherwise would probably require rewiring his brain.
- He says embarrassing things in public. Unless he's telling a joke that will put a friend into therapy for twenty years, it's not a big deal.

In order to keep your relationship healthy, you both have to learn to let some of your peeves slide. Otherwise you'll spend most of your time bickering about issues that really don't matter much. Don't expect absolute perfection from your partner. Just stick to your guns about the things that are really important to you, and the rest of the time, put on headphones and turn up the music.

> Conflict cannot survive without your participation.
>
> WAYNE DYER

Red Flags

A chapter on conflict is not complete without bringing up a few red flags. Red flags are those issues, behaviors, and attitudes that are absolutely nonnegotiable. They are problems you should *never* let go under *any* circumstances—like physical abuse, verbal abuse, and insidious addictions and habits. If you ignore them, these red flags will, without a doubt, destroy your relationship and possibly your life. The only thing you can do when they are present is get out of the relationship as soon as possible. Unfortunately, many women in these situations find it difficult to get out because they are emotionally and financially connected to the guy. Often, it takes help from a trained professional to make the choice to get out of the relationship.

The subject of abuse is large enough to fill volumes and volumes of books, so we can't possibly cover all of the related topics here, but we will touch upon some of the major red flags and symptoms of an abusive relationship. If you need more information, you can call the National Domestic Violence Hotline at 1-800-799-SAFE (or 1-800-799-7233) to get help and find out about local organizations in your area.

Red Flag #1: Physical Abuse

Physical abuse often starts off small—insults here and there, a little push, or maybe even a slap in the face. Then it escalates over time into a far more dangerous situation. Sometimes abusers don't seem dangerous in the beginning. They appear charming, handsome, and interesting. But they slowly reveal an angry, controlling side. They often apologize after an abusive incident, so many women are tempted to forgive their abuser, even in the most dire of situations. This is what the experts call a "cycle of abuse," where victims are hit, they forgive their abuser, and then he does it again. They don't want to give up their dream of a happy, normal relationship, so they keep believing he will change. If a guy acts this way, nothing you do will make him change. You are in a physically abusive relationship if:

- He has ever, even once, punched you, kicked you, threw you up against a wall, or threatened you in any way.
- He has inflicted any type of physical injury whatsoever, including stepping on you or pushing you to the ground.
- He threatens to kill you or someone you love. Take these threats seriously. Many women don't take threats seriously and they miss the opportunity to protect themselves and their loved ones.
- You feel like you are in danger when you are with him.
- He takes things of yours and ruins them because he is trying to control you. He might ruin nice clothing you have because he says it's slutty. He might destroy pictures you have of other men you've dated or of guy friends in your life.

Sometimes men who are abusive in relationships act very sweet in their interactions with those outside the relationship. So don't rely on what other people think about your relationship to make a decision. Just because your mother says, "He's so cute," or your sister says, "Oh, I just love him. He's a sweetie," doesn't mean you are wrong if you think he's being abusive. Listen to your own instincts and trust your own judgment when it comes to the men you date. If you suspect a friend is in an abusive relationship, you might hear her make excuses like the following:

- He hits me only when he's drunk, but he's very sweet when he's sober.
- He always apologizes, so I'm not concerned.

- It's not that bad. He only pushes me around once in a while.
- When he has a hard day at work, he can't help it.
- As long as no one else knows, it's not a big deal.
- I know it's going to stop once we're married.
- It's my fault. I always egg him on and I can be pretty nasty.

Every day, people settle for less than they deserve. They are only partially living or at best living a partial life.

BO BENNETT

Red Flag #2: Verbal Abuse

Many people don't realize that words can be just as damaging as physical abuse. Verbal abuse takes a toll on your happiness, health, and self-esteem. It often escalates into physical abuse as the relationship progresses. There are several different types of verbal abuse, but all of them will make you feel insecure, unloved, and controlled. You are being verbally abused if:

- He insults you and ridicules you. He makes you feel like nothing you do is right.
- You are always walking on eggshells around him because he flies off the handle so easily.
- He tries to control you by keeping you from your friends and family, telling you what to wear or how to cut your hair.
- He tries to control you through money. He spends your money or uses his own to manipulate you.

- He denies your reality. When you confront him with things that are bothering you, he always says he doesn't have any idea what you're talking about.
- He makes constant demands. You always think if you fulfill his needs he'll love you more, but he always comes up with new demands.
- He doesn't show you love or affection.
- He has very unpredictable mood swings, going from being very nice to nasty and mean.
- You never really feel like you "connect" with him. He just doesn't seem to understand how his behavior is affecting you or why it's wrong.

This list is not inclusive, but it does contain many of the most obvious signs of verbal abuse. To find out more about this type of abuse, you can read *The Verbally Abusive Relationship* by Patricia Evans. Remember that verbal abuse is just as dangerous as physical abuse, but sometimes it's more difficult to recognize. A relationship cannot survive if this type of abuse is present.

Red Flag #3: Other Forms of Abuse and Addictions

Other, less obvious forms of abuse include addictions and habits that destroy a relationship. If he chooses a certain lifestyle and it is detrimental to your health and happiness, that's abuse. You should not have to live with the consequences of his bad choices. You should not have to support his habits and suffer because of them. If any of these issues are present in your relationship, they, too, are reason to call things off. They include:

- An addiction to prescription or street drugs
- A mental illness that he refuses to seek help for
- Alcoholism
- A criminal offense or jail time for a behavior that doesn't go away, like rape or assault
- A gambling or spending addiction
- A child pornography fetish
- An addiction to sex or strange sexual games

Sometimes men develop a problem once you've been with them for years. Many women want to intervene and help their guy because they've invested so much time and energy into the relationship. But most of these problems require professional intervention, and even then, sometimes a person just can't change. The longer you stay in a relationship where abuse is present, the harder it will be to get out. But you cannot have a meaningful, long-term relationship with someone who abuses you. The only right answer is to remove yourself from the situation and move on with your life.

> No person is your friend who demands your silence, or denies your right to grow.
>
> ALICE WALKER

For a relationship to work, fighting has to be constructive. It is a chance for both people to air their grievances and develop a better understanding of each other. Couples have their own unique ways of fighting and their own tolerance level for certain types of behaviors. But regardless of these differences, abuse is never present in a strong, successful relationship. After you fight and make up, you should feel like you've grown closer, not further apart. You should feel a sense of goodwill, not negativity. So pay attention to the fights you and your guy have, ask the right questions, and use the answers to help you decide whether or not your relationship is really worth fighting for.

chapter five

Just the Two
of Us

A time comes in every relationship when a gradual shift occurs in the way two people relate to each other and in how they are viewed by the outside world. They are no longer just casually dating. They are a full-fledged couple. They become a unit that attends parties together, grocery shops together, spends cozy Friday nights together, and even celebrates holidays together.

You might notice that other people start treating you like you're a couple before you even have the chance feel like one yourself. Perhaps the customs lady at the airport assumes you're married. Or your mom sends you coupons to get a photo taken together at the mall. When these little things start to happen, you can't help but feel like you're crossing over into uncharted territory. He's no longer just some guy you see on occasion. He's your *boyfriend* and you're a *couple* to your friends, your family, and to everybody else out there. You're officially spoken for, and that realization can be a little bit scary.

It's normal to go through a period of questioning when you feel this "couple status" take hold. You might ask, "Is this what I want? How will my life change? Do we really belong together? Are we good as a couple?" For your relationship to be successful long-term, you have to be able to answer these questions, embrace couplehood, and welcome both the excitement and the responsibility that come along with it.

Turning into a Twosome

Turning into a twosome can be really fun. You're thrilled to do "couple stuff" like walking together through the park or shopping in Home Depot. You have a picture of the two of you prominently displayed on your desk at work and maybe you even sent out holiday cards signed by both of you. Rigid, planned, formal dates are a thing of the distant past, and you spend your time hanging out casually and even running errands together. He becomes your everyday buddy.

Take a step back and think about all of those ways you're a couple now. Does this new label make you happy or a little uncomfortable? Are you generally embracing the idea or do you feel like telling your friends to knock off the "his and hers" gifts and leave him out of the picture? Pay attention to how you feel about these changes. Your feelings will help you determine whether or not you're really happy with him by your side.

Signs of a Shift

When you become a couple, you start trusting each other as friends and you begin to act in a way that indicates you're committed to each other. At first the signs of commitment will be small. You might sign up for a gym membership together or give each other designated closet space at your respective apartments. But in doing so, you're indicating that you want to become more a part of each other's lives. Think about those things you've done to encourage the shift to couplehood. If you can't think of very many, it might be a sign that you've been resisting this change, or that he has, and then you have to ask yourself why. Signs of the shift to couplehood might include:

- Diving into the "couples culture" by arranging dinners with other coupled or married friends and taking vacations to romantic destinations
- Sharing your less glamorous self and the items that go along with it, like razors, toothpaste, towels, and even a toothbrush (yuck!)
- Signing up for a Sam's Club or Costco membership together and spending weekends shopping for household things
- Sharing ownership of a pet, an electronic gizmo, or anything else you both value
- Calling yourself "mom and dad" to that cat or dog you share
- Attending the Blueberry Festival, Strawberry Festival, street art show, and the Polish church bizarre just like all the old married people do
- Replying to a friend's e-mails or voicemails on behalf of one another
- Chatting with each other's siblings and parents

- Putting the other person down as an emergency contact
- Calling each other from work, when you're traveling, or on holidays if you don't spend them together
- Doing each other's laundry, making dinner, and just generally "playing house"

If these little things are not happening, or if they are but you feel horribly uncomfortable with them, he is not the right guy for you, or you're not ready to commit to him just yet. These changes are a natural part of the evolution of every relationship. If they aren't present, it's a sign that you are not growing closer to him and welcoming him into your everyday world.

The Rest of the World

For a while you might feel annoyed if people don't address you as a unit and freaked out when they do. It's normal to be a little confused as you leave behind some of the things you love about being single and embrace this new phase in your relationship. Eventually, however, you should be okay with these changes. You have to be able to accept him as an extension of you, someone who is your other half. You should feel happy to have him by your side and enjoy being known as his girlfriend. And he should feel the same way. You should be excited when:

- The wedding invitation is no longer addressed to you and "guest." Now it has his name on it too.

- Your parents send him a birthday gift and they call him to see how he's doing even when you're not around.
- Married friends say things to you like, "When the two of you get married . . ." or "Some day when you two have kids . . ."
- Old friends from high school say things like, "I never thought you would end up with a yuppie type like [insert your guy's name]" or "Isn't it nice that after all these years of dating, you've finally met *the one*."
- People assume you agree with his opinions and share his interests. He's a Democrat so they think you are too or he likes the outdoors so they think you're both into hiking.
- Friends always invite both of you to events. You no longer have to ask if you can bring him.
- His friends call you "The Mrs." and other "wifely" names.
- You no longer get as many individual gifts for holidays. You get one gift for both of you and it's a kitchen gadget.
- His sister asks you to be in her wedding and asks you what kind of bridesmaid dresses you plan to pick for yours.

If you can't come to terms with being known as a couple to the outside world, he is not the right guy for you or you might just have trouble with the idea of commitment (which will be addressed in Chapter 9). Either way, you aren't ready just yet to give this guy your ring finger.

Becoming a Team

There's more to being a couple than sharing toothpaste, DVDs, and friends. At some point, these smaller connections between you blossom into more significant ones that show you're committed to each other on a meaningful level. You're a team and that means you care about your team member, you support him, and you want to see him happy. He feels the same way about you. The two of you work together to tackle life's challenges and support one another in the same way close friends do. Do you and your boyfriend act like a team? In other words, do you show your commitment to one another in little ways every day? Some of the things you might do include:

> Ultimately, being a part of a team means competing, working, living, and winning and losing together.
>
> STEVE KERR

Putting Each Other First

You should notice that now sometimes you're putting each other first above your own needs and the needs of friends and family. For example, perhaps you used to go out at night even if he was sick, but now you feel like you should stick around and take care of him. He does the same when you have the sniffles. Of course, neither of you is a selfless saint. But on the whole, you look out for each other. You're willing to sacrifice your own needs to make the other person happy. You do things like:

- Use your vacation days to help him move to a new apartment
- Let him have the last mozzarella stick

- Reschedule commitments that fall on his birthday
- Buy the stuff you think he'll like when you're at the grocery store
- Take time to call him when you're out late with friends just so he doesn't worry
- Make his Super Bowl party extra special even though you're not a fan of all the guys he invited
- Wrap his gift in the expensive paper you've been saving for a special occasion
- Let him play his favorite CD in the car
- Tweeze the sliver out of his foot even though it's really gross

The relationship is not a one-way street. He makes sacrifices for you as well. You both anticipate each other's needs, and you enjoy making each other happy. You value each other and the relationship enough to invest extra time and energy into it.

> I figure that the degree of difficulty in combining two lives ranks somewhere between rerouting a hurricane and finding a parking place in downtown Manhattan.
>
> CLAIRE CLONINGER

Supporting One Another

You should also notice that you're supporting each other like friends on a day-to-day basis. If you have a goal you are working toward, he supports it and sends you little articles to help you achieve it. If he's trying to save money to buy a new car, you encourage him and take an interest in his progress. You realize that being on the same team means that you have to support and defend each other to win. So you do things like:

- Try to make him feel better after he loses his important basketball game
- Stick up for him when your sister says he's too much of a jokester
- Offer him constructive criticism to help him improve his cooking skills
- Share with him your stock market or fitness secrets
- Cheer for him when he gets a promotion
- Make an effort to understand why he dislikes one of your friends
- Refrain from correcting him in public so you don't embarrass him
- Help other people understand his decisions or opinions when they don't agree with him

And he does these things for you too. You're loyal to each other and you want to protect each other. So you prop each other up. You know you're stronger as a unit than you are apart so you work together to accomplish life's tasks.

> A good band is like a team. You want to have the right balance. It's not always the best people you need, but the right ones for the job.
>
> RONNIE HAWKINS

Testing the Twosome

You might not be able to see all the ways you're working as a team—or not—until you face a few challenges together. As you work through problems, you learn either that your two-man team is invincible or that you desperately need to find a new partner. Think about the challenges that you and your guy have faced. Did you work together to get through them? Do you feel like they made you stronger? Or are you certain that if you ever have to face the same thing again, it will rip you apart? It's not enough to love and support each other on the good days. For your relationship to work over the long haul, you have to be able to survive and even thrive in the face of some very grueling challenges. Can your relationship survive life's biggest tests?

> Sympathy constitutes friendship; but in love there is a sort of antipathy, or opposing. Each strives to be the other, and both together make up one whole.
>
> SAMUEL TAYLOR COLERIDGE

Level One Challenges: The Little Things

Level one challenges are the smaller trials, the little things that happen in daily life. For example, your cat flips out and scratches his arms or his favorite dry cleaner ruins your expensive shirt. These things won't kill you, but they introduce a lot of stress into your partnership. If you don't learn to deal with level one challenges effectively, they will act like little pins needling their way between the two of you. They might seem harmless at first, but the way you tackle them together is important because they never go away. Daily life will certainly never be challenge-free. Take some time to think about the problems and annoyances you face daily and how you deal with them when you're together. Can your relationship survive these little stresses?

Household Issues

Case 1: One evening you find several large black spiders in your bathroom and you call him in a panic. Does he come over and help you exterminate? Does he make you laugh by leaving a picture of Spiderman taped to the medicine cabinet? Or does he tell you he's pretty busy but he hopes you find the right bug spray at the grocery store?

Case 2: How about when his car breaks down—do you offer to drive him everywhere until he can get it fixed? Or do you send him a monthly bus pass, cross your fingers, and hope he makes it to work?

The Challenge: Frustrating things happen around the house all the time. The air-conditioning breaks in ninety-degree heat. The refrigerator quits the night before your dinner party. Do the two of you help each other through these stressful problems? You should feel like he's on your side and there to make life easier. You should want to be there to help him even when it's not convenient. These unexpected everyday problems are a true test of whether or not you support each other and you have to pass with flying colors for your relationship to thrive.

Driving

Case 1: You're still finishing up the six-hour car ride that should have been only three. You've been taking turns reading maps, getting lost, and asking scary gas station attendants for help. You've pulled over at least a half-dozen times to yell at each other. Do you end up staying at an eerie motel because communication broke down or do you work together to get to your destination? Do you blame him for the fact that you got lost or do you feel bad that he was stuck behind the wheel all that time?

Case 2: The traffic is unbearable, the sun is hot, and you're stuck together in a motionless line of tractor trailers. You're late for your parents' wedding anniversary party and supposed to give the opening speech. Do you start yelling at each other and become irrational or do you research other routes you can take to get there? Do you flip out because no one knows you're going to be late or does he jump out and ask the driver next to you if he can borrow his cell phone to call your sister?

The Challenge: Something about being in a car challenges couples like nothing else does. While your drives may not be without arguments, you should work out some way to make trips a little less stressful. When surprises pop up, you should move into solution mode, not start yelling at each other. Driving is an important test of how well you divide up tasks and work together to solve a problem. This skill is an essential one you must learn if you want your relationship to last.

Vacations

Case 1: You decide to go away for a week together. You are dying to stay in a bed and breakfast on the Italian countryside.

He wants to go to Costa Rica and windsurf. How long does it take to agree on the destination, and how many arguments do you have in the process? When one person wins, do you then decide to go to the other destination the following year? When you arrive at that shoddy bungalow on the beach, do you smile as you swiftly remove the giant green beetle from the door or do you scream at him for getting you into this mess?

Case 2: He wants to spend his week off at a cottage in the mountains with his friends. You were under the impression that the two of you would spend some time together. Does he figure out a way to make it up to you? Do you come up with a way to spend part of the vacation together and part of it with friends so you're both happy? Or does he tell you to calm down and then head off into the wilderness with his buddies?

The Challenge: You should be able to enjoy your time off together in a way that makes you both happy. One person shouldn't always dictate how things are going to be. It's okay if you don't agree, but you should both be willing to work toward a compromise. Vacation time presents an opportunity for you to learn to balance each other's interests and preferences with your own, a skill you must learn if you want your relationship to last.

Job Stress

Case 1: You have a huge project due, a cold, and severe menstrual cramps. Your computer knocks you offline and you lose the most recent changes to your document. Do you come home at night, unleash, and take out all of your frustrations on him? Do you tell him that if he would only earn more money and marry you, you wouldn't have to work at this stupid job anymore? Or do you drink hot cocoa, go to bed early, and wake up the next day with a more optimistic outlook?

Case 2: His boss is breathing down his neck every day and just keeps piling on the work. He's been staying late and getting in early, so he's exhausted. Does he just stop paying attention to you and offer no explanation? Or does he go to the gym, work off his stress, and then call you and explain to you that he's just not in the best of moods because of his job?

The Challenge: While most of us slip up on occasion and take out our stress on the person we love, you should be able to recognize you're doing it or at least admit that you did it after the fact. Both of you have to learn to take life's frustrations out in a healthy way instead of on each other. This skill will help keep your relationship strong.

> The romantic love we feel toward the opposite sex is probably one extra help from God to bring you together, but that's it. All the rest of it, the true love, is the test.
>
> JOAN CHEN

Level Two Challenges: The Bigger Tests

Do you feel exhausted from reading through those challenges? And just think, those are only the small ones. When level two challenges arise, the stakes are higher, the issues are bigger, and the outcome is more meaningful. Can your relationship survive level two challenges? Can you find a way to stay together despite the added pressure they create? Read on and find out.

A Major Move

Case 1: He is trying to figure out if he wants to accept a new job across the country or one nearby. You don't want to move because you love the city you live in. Do you both talk openly about your feelings, hopes, and reservations or do you distance yourself from each other? Does he agree to take the job and say something vague like "I'll e-mail you" or does he present a detailed schedule of when and how he plans to see you?

Case 2: You've been dating for years and now your lease is coming due. You're kind of hoping to move in with him. Do you feel comfortable talking to him about the situation or do you drop hints by leaving your lease renewal forms near his work bag?

The Challenge: When you're dating, an impending move will force both of you to reassess the relationship and define clearly what you want out of it. If you don't feel comfortable communicating about an issue like this one, you will have problems talking about other big issues down the road. You must be able to communicate openly about all issues for the relationship to survive.

Family Stress

Case 1: His sister is hogging all of his time lately, bugging him to help her paint her apartment and insisting that he attend every family event on the calendar. You feel neglected, and a little left out. Does he understand how you feel and make more of an effort to include you? Or does he tell you that no one is as important as his family and then expect you to understand?

Case 2: Your father seems to be a little skeptical of him. He picks on him a lot and sometimes it sounds mean. You know your Dad is just jealous that you have a new man in your life, but can your guy understand that? Do you care about your guy enough to ask your Dad to stop giving him a hard time?

The Challenge: Many relationships break up because the two people cannot get along with each other's families. Your relationship with each other should be a priority even if you are close with your family. That doesn't mean that your family is unimportant. It just means that you must learn to listen to each other's concerns, and take them seriously, while also maintaining your relationship with your family. It might seem like an impossible challenge, but it's one all couples must master to keep their relationship alive.

Health Problems

Case 1: When you met each other you were in perfect health. But one day, you get a call from him and he's wheezing into the phone. You go over to his place to see how he is and he's coughing up phlegm. He used to be really attractive but now he looks a little different. Do you think he's adorable anyway just because he's still trying to pick on you between coughs? Do you feel like you would stick your hand in his mouth and plug up that postnasal drip if you could? (Okay, maybe no one would go that far!)

Case 2: You've had a bump on your arm forever and you have no idea why. Finally you go to the doctor, and she tells you that you need to have it removed and tested for different diseases. Does he research it online and tell you all the harmless things it might be or does he let you convince yourself that it's deadly? Is he there for you the day you're going to find out the results or does he tell you to text him and let him know how it went?

The Challenge: The human body is certainly not glamorous most of the time. When you're young and dating, your problems are pretty minor compared to what you will face as you age. If you can't help each other through minor sicknesses, health scares, and other issues now, your relationship will eventually face a big health challenge you can't overcome. The ability to handle the gross and unattractive side of each other is critical to the long-term success of your relationship.

Money and Spending

Case 1: You love to save money and he's always blowing his cash on new gadgets for his apartment. You know it's his money, but you worry that he's being frivolous with it. Do you talk to him about it or just let him spend like a maniac? Is he receptive to your advice and reasoning or does he get angry with you for butting in?

Case 2: Your friend needs a loan or she can't pay for her last semester of graduate school. You've agreed to give her $5,000 out of your savings. He thinks you're crazy and tells you that she'll never pay you back. He suggests you draw up a legal contract to make sure you get repaid. Do you listen to his concerns and take them seriously or do you just go ahead with the loan?

The Challenge: Dealing with money is one of the biggest issues couples face. But if you end up together, you will have to agree on how to spend it, how much to spend, and how to invest what's left. If you can't have an open discussion about finances and agree with each other on these issues when you're dating, you will not be able to do so when the money belongs to both of you. You must be able to reach some level of agreement on financial issues for your relationship to succeed.

Time

Case 1: You're so busy with your job that you only have time to see him once a week. He is starting to feel neglected. Do you make an extra effort to fit him into your day or do you tell him he's being a baby and hope the problem will go away?

Case 2: Lately he's spending more and more time with his friends. When he's not out with them, they are over at his place hanging out with the two of you. You're starting to feel like he's dating his buddies and you're the third wheel. Do you express your need for more alone time or just suck it up and start going out with your friends more often? Does he do special things to remind you that he still loves you more than he loves them or does he just forget about you and take you for granted?

The Challenge: You know exactly how you like to spend your time and what portion of it you want to allocate to your relationships, your job, your workout, and your leisure activities. The problem is that he has an idea of how he likes to spend his time too and your schedules don't always gel. Many couples break up because they can't agree on how much time they should spend together, how often they should have sex, and how they define "quality" couple time. You need to feel comfortable discussing these issues while you're dating. If you want to keep your relationship alive, you both have to feel satisfied with the time and attention you're receiving from the other person.

> My wife and I tried two or three times in the last 40 years to have breakfast together, but it was so disagreeable we had to stop.
>
> WINSTON CHURCHILL

Temptation

Case 1: You just hired a new employee. He's only three years your junior, and he's adorable. You really enjoy working with him and sometimes you lose track of time because he's so much fun. Do you act on your interest or at least keep flirting? Or do you recognize that what you're doing could be threatening your relationship and work to put some distance between you and the new guy?

Case 2: Your guy has been getting home late at night and offering no explanation. He's traveling more and he is generally unavailable. You suspect that he might be cheating on you. Do you confront him or wait and see what happens? When you do confront him, does he offer a good explanation for his weird behavior or is he vague?

The Challenge: Both you and your guy will face moments in life when you are tempted by someone else. The real question is whether you will act on that temptation. While you can't chain each other up to prevent one another from cheating, you can talk to each other about infidelity and temptation.

You can make sure you agree that cheating is a deal breaker, something you cannot tolerate under any circumstances. The temptations you face while you're dating present a great opportunity to discuss big issues of trust and to clarify what you expect from your partner.

Sticking together through all of these trials that pop up is not at all easy. It requires patience, communication, and compromise on every level. But you should welcome these challenges. If you face enough of them while you're dating, you'll get a real flavor for how you would work together if you were married. In the end, if you can't deal with life's challenges successfully, you can't survive as a couple and you shouldn't continue moving forward in the relationship.

> If I know a guy is cheating on his wife, I don't trust him in the boardroom or on the golf course. You're either a cheater or you're not. With cheating, there's no middle ground.
>
> JAMES, AGE 46

Off Days

Being a twosome means working together as a team to tackle the challenges that life throws your way. It means looking out for each other and supporting one another. But it doesn't mean you're attached at the hip and you share a brain. There will be days when you just want to do your own thing without him. Likewise, he'll have days when he feels that way about you. There will be times when you don't agree and moments when you don't feel in love. These "off days" are a normal part of every relationship.

Your off days are a problem only if:
- They happen six out of seven days a week.
- They get increasingly worse over time and eventually you don't even want to see his face.
- They are caused by a much larger, fundamental problem in your relationship. For instance, you don't feel like you're getting enough love and affection, so you don't want to give any to him.
- You aren't just lacking that "loving feeling," you've got that "hating feeling." You actually want to hurt him or be mean to him on your off days.
- You aren't there for him on days when he really needs you.
- You get mad at him when he has an off day and wants to be alone.
- You spend your off days with another guy.
- You don't balance out your off days with "on days" where you make an effort to show him how much you care.

> The hardest of all is learning to be a well of affection, and not a fountain; to show them we love them not when we feel like it, but when they do.
>
> NAN FAIRBROTHER

Some women love to spend time alone and they really enjoy shopping solo or entertaining themselves. Other women are particularly sensitive to PMS or work stress and when it hits, they just want to be alone. If one of these conditions describes you, you might have more off days than some other women do. It's important to find a guy who is the same way, someone who appreciates and respects your need to do your own thing and have time away from him. Otherwise, you will constantly be at odds because he will feel neglected.

When you agree to be a twosome, you accept responsibility for the way your attitude and actions impact the other person. You start thinking more about what is important to your partner and you work harder to arrive at compromises that make you both happy. Often you have to meet half way and give up something that's important to you to come to an agreement. The ultimate challenge you'll face in your relationship is determining when to be your own person and when to work together, deciding when to give something up and when to stand your ground. Being a couple requires hard work and sacrifice, but you still have to make time to take care of yourself. If you don't continue to do the things you need to do to feel good about your life, you won't have the energy you need to invest in the relationship.

People often say that you know you've met 'the one' when you can't imagine your life without him. But most of us cherish our alone time and wouldn't mind if he went away for a week or two. The real question is, do you want him to come back, and do you want him to come back in one piece?

VANESSA, AGE 35

chapter six

Who Is
This Guy?

When you meet a guy, he already has a long, varied history, one that has firmly established his personality. He brings into the relationship his past, his experiences, his preferences, and his peeves. All of these things make him the person he is, and most of these elements won't change even after you've been dating him for years. So once you get to know him, it's important to take a step back and evaluate him as an individual, out of the context of the relationship. Ask yourself questions like, "Do I respect this guy? Do I like him as a person? Would he be someone I would want in my life as a friend even if there were no romance between us?"

The answers to these questions are imperative because in order to have a successful long-term relationship, you need to be able to trust him with many aspects of your life, from issues as simple as paying a phone bill, to matters as complex as caring for your elderly parents. You have to know he's a good person through and through, and that the qualities you respect in him are fundamental to who he is, enduring traits that you can rely on for life. In other words, for the relationship to succeed, you have to like the person he is on his own just as much as you like the person he is when he's with you.

A Hint of Hero

We've seen it happen dozens of times on television: a woman shows up at a restaurant for girls' night out, sits down at the table, and flashes her girlfriends a love-struck grin. Then one of them asks the inevitable question, *"Who is he?"* Usually she answers the way any of us would. She tells her friends his name and how wonderful he is. Maybe she mentions his job or where she met him. But she doesn't have the real scoop yet, the meaningful details about who he is and what he stands for. She can't yet answer questions like, Is he trustworthy? Is he honest? Is he caring? What is his personality like? But eventually, when she gets to know him, she has to answer these questions so she can decide what kind of long-term partner he'll make.

How well can you answer these questions about your guy? Do you know who he is, *really*?

The Good-Guy Dictionary

Think about the traits of a "good guy," they are those fundamental qualities we value in our friends, family members, and significant others. They are the characteristics we admire in a hero, and the things our parents and teachers hope we become. It's important that a guy behaves well when he's with other people—his family, friends, and even strangers—not just when he's with you. So first, focus on how he treats others. Later in the chapter, you'll have the chance to ask the same questions again, with a focus on how he treats you. Does your guy have good-guy traits? Use the "good-guy dictionary" to find out.

car·ing (adj.):
Feeling and exhibiting concern and empathy for others

Does he feel bad when he reads a story about impoverished communities? Would he stop and help a hurt cat or dog or would he ignore it and keep going? If a friend of his was injured, would he go to the hospital to visit him? Does your guy put himself in other people's shoes and feel their pain?

Remember: Sometimes he might not feel like being caring, but you'll still need him to care about you, your family, and your life. If he thinks it's important to be a caring person, he will be, regardless of his mood or circumstances.

sup·por·tive (adj.):
Furnishing support or assistance

Does he offer to carry the old lady's groceries or open the door for the person who can't quite do it? Does he help his sister edit her resume or offer to shovel the neighbor's sidewalk when it snows? Is he generally a helpful person most of the time or does he try to wiggle out of extra work?

Remember: Sometimes he'll feel moody and tired and he won't feel like supporting you. He might be angry with you and feel like you're annoying him. Nevertheless, you'll still need him to be there for you, and if he thinks it's important to be a supportive person, he will be.

hon·est (adj.):
Not deceptive or fraudulent; genuine

Does he tell people what they want to hear or is he up front about his feelings? Does he have a history of lying to friends or family about his income or his lifestyle? How would he react if a friend lied? Does he comment on stories about lying and cheating in the news? Does he think honesty is important?

Remember: At times, he'll feel tempted to lie about silly things and maybe even serious issues. He might feel like spending a little too much money on his poker game or going to a strip club with the guys, and he'll think, "What she doesn't know won't hurt her." But, if he values honesty, he will be up front with you about things that affect you no matter what.

loy·al (adj.):
Faithful to a person, ideal, custom, cause, or duty

Does he show allegiance to his alma mater? Is he loyal to his friends or does he cut them down when they aren't around? How does he react when he hears about men being unfaithful to their wives or guys cheating at work? Does he have customs or values he remains committed to even when someone challenges them?

Remember: Other women will cross his path and he will find them attractive. If he values loyalty, he'll remain faithful to you even when these other opportunities come his way.

re·spon·si·ble (adj.):
Able to make moral or rational decisions on one's own;
able to answer for one's behavior

Does he pay his bills on time or is he repeatedly late? Do his friends ever ask him for help moving because they know they can count on him? Does he show up for important events on time? Does he hold a steady job? Does he take care of his health? Is he generally a responsible person?

Remember: Sometimes he'll feel terribly lazy. He might even wish he could quit his job and skip town. But if he's a responsible person, he'll do all of the things he should be doing to make the relationship work even when his heart isn't in it.

pa·tient (adj.):
Tolerant; understanding; bearing or enduring pain,
difficulty, provocation, or annoyance with calmness

Does he respond calmly when a car pulls in front of him on the highway or does he flip out and start yelling? Is he patient with his family and friends? Is he short-tempered when someone overcharges him or does he deal with the situation calmly?

Remember: Once in a while when he's angry with you and you've pushed his last button, he'll want to explode. But if he's generally a patient person, these frustrating moments won't always turn into a fight. He'll let things go and deal with his stress in other ways.

brave (adj.):
Possessing or displaying courage; valiant

Does he speak up for himself even when he's nervous about making waves? Does he start a new job or take a business risk when he knows it is right to do so, even if he's scared? Everyone feels fear at times, but does he let his fear cripple him or does he work against it to make his life what he wants it to be?

Remember: Relationships do require bravery. He might need to defend you to his mother or stick up for you when the car repairman tries to sell you a $5,000 muffler. He'll also need to feel brave enough to tell you his feelings and have open discussions about important issues. If he's a courageous person in other parts of his life, you'll be able to count on him being brave in your relationship too.

self·less (adj.):
Having, exhibiting, or motivated by no concern for oneself;
unselfish

Does he let people go in front of him in the deli line even when he's hungry or does he push his way to the front? Would he give his piece of pizza to the homeless man even if he didn't have any money left to buy another one? Does he do things for other people even when it's not convenient? Or is he more like a spoiled brat, stomping his feet if he doesn't get his own way?

Remember: Sometimes he'll want nothing more than to be left alone. He won't want to help you with the dishes or the groceries or kids or listen to how your day was. But if he's generally an unselfish person, he'll still put your needs first when it really matters.

It's important that the guy you're dating is a good person at heart, and that means that you would approve of the way he behaves even if you weren't dating him, even if he were just some guy you were watching through a one-way mirror. That doesn't mean he has to behave perfectly every second of every day. Sometimes bad situations or annoying people do bring out the worst in all of us. But he should behave well most of the time. It's easy for a man to be loving and supportive when he first meets you and wants to impress you, but he won't remain that way for long if it's not part of who he is at the core. And for those days when he's driving you nuts and you feel like leaving him, you'll put the extra effort in to work on the relationship if you respect him as a person. So evaluate your guy and make sure you can check off these positive qualities before you move forward in the relationship.

Hard times don't create heroes. It is during the hard times when the 'hero' within us is revealed.

BOB RILEY

downstream Keep in mind that you're downstream in the relationship and that means everything he does upstream when you're not around trickles your way and affects you. Here are a few examples of this phenomenon offered by real women:

- "My ex-husband was an alcoholic and to him, drinking always came first before me and our child. One day I paid all of our bills and then gave him the rest of the money to deposit at the bank in a savings account. He never made it to the bank. He spent it all at a bar on alcohol."—*Ann, age 54*

- "I never realized how much people judge you based on the person you're with until I married Rob. He's so friendly and outgoing and everyone always just assumes I'm the same way. They love him, so they automatically embrace me because I'm his wife."—*Kristin, age 38*

- "When I was dating Chris, I always thought he was a pushover. He would go to the ends of the earth to help a friend even if the guy was a jerk. But now I realize that his kindness is a wonderful asset to our marriage. No matter how mad he is at me, he never stops caring or doing the things he should be doing to keep our relationship alive."—*Rebecca, age 34*

- "I'm a spiteful person and sometimes when I'm angry with Jim I am so tempted to ruin his favorite DVD or rip up the money in his wallet. But I always manage to hold back because I know in my heart that he would never in a million years do those things to me or to anyone for that matter."—*Marie, age 39*

- "Tom is an optimist. Everything he comes in contact with is a little bit happier when he gets done with it. It's like he has this cloud of positive energy surrounding him. I'm the complete opposite. I get down and really negative when things don't go my way. But fortunately, his optimism rubs off on me when I need it most."—*Nancy, age 28*

- "I know I can trust Matt to take care of my dog when I'm gone and to water my plants. I know that if the day comes when we have kids, he'll take care of them too, even if I'm not around to tell him what to do. He's just a very caring, responsible person and it gives me peace of mind to know that these qualities are a part of who he is regardless of whether or not I'm in his life."—*Gwen, age 27*

- "I used to have to hound Doug to pay his cable bill and take out his garbage. At first it didn't bother me, but eventually I had to invest so much energy to get him to do even little things that I was truly exhausted. If a guy isn't willing to take responsibility for his own life, you can't make him do it and he's certainly never going to take responsibility for yours."—*Michele, age 35*

- "When Mike is in a good mood, he is the sweetest person. But when he gets angry, his most primitive instincts kick in and he becomes this extremely impatient, nasty person. Fortunately, even his really bad side isn't all that bad. I've seen him unveil his worst and it's really not scary in the least. So I'm confident that our worst fights in our relationship will never be something I can't handle."—*Kyra, age 31*

The "Enough" Rule

Though it's important for your guy to be a good person, he doesn't have to be a saint. No one is perfect all the time, and we all have a different idea of just how responsible or caring or loyal a person should be. For instance, you might have zero tolerance for dishonesty and someone else might think little white lies are no big deal. Or while many of us are impatient when we're in traffic, you might feel like you can't handle a man who has a short fuse in any situation. So ultimately, it's up to you to decide what these qualities mean to you, which ones are critical, and which ones you can live without.

Once you've identified your critical qualities, remember that they come in different shades, meaning a person isn't either honest or not honest. He can be "kind of honest" or "honest most of the time." So your critical qualities just have to be *enough* a part of who he is to make you happy. In other words, he doesn't have to be exceedingly responsible. He just has to be responsible *enough* to satisfy you. He doesn't have to have endless patience for everyone all the time. He just has to be patient *enough* to make you happy. You have to decide what "enough" means to you, but here are some guidelines.

100% Caring: He stops to help every old person in sight and he uses his apartment as a refuge for homeless kittens.
Caring Enough: He forgets his mother's birthday, but he does remember to send a huge bouquet a few days late.

100% Supportive: He shows up for his best friend's knee surgery and sits in the waiting room all night.

Supportive Enough: He takes a trip to the hospital once the guy is in the recovery room and drops off one of his favorite magazines.

100% Honest: He tells his sister about her surprise party because he can't bear the thought of lying to her.
Honest Enough: He drops her hints so she knows enough to put on a cute dress before she shows up.

100% Loyal: He won't stop loaning his buddy money even though the guy never pays him back.
Loyal Enough: He gives him one last $100 bill with a note taped to it that says, "Get a job already."

100% Responsible: He's the designated driver for all of his friends all the time. Some of them even call him when he's not at the party with them.
Responsible Enough: He calls a cab for his drunk buddies if they need it and pays the driver to get them home safely.

100% Patient: He calmly walks down the street behind the slow-moving crowd. He stops when they stop and he moves when they move.
Patient Enough: He calmly walks behind the old man who can't go any faster, but gives the chatty preteens a dirty look and brushes by them as fast as he can.

100% Brave: He stops the robbers with his own hands and fights them until they put down the lady's purse.
Brave Enough: He agrees to testify against them in their trial even though they give him threatening looks the whole time.

100% Selfless: He lets everyone stay at his apartment whenever they want to—friends, family, and even an occasional random person he doesn't know very well.

Selfless Enough: He lets his best friends sleep on his couch as long as they bring their own toiletries.

The hardest thing about the "enough rule" is that it is so subjective. Even you might change your mind about what you think it means to be "caring enough" or "selfless enough." But you should be able to tell very easily if he isn't caring at all or if he's 100 percent selfish. If you do notice that these negative elements are overwhelmingly present in his personality, it should set off alarms in your head. It's tough, if not impossible, to have a successful relationship with someone who just isn't at all a good person. A long-term commitment is such a serious and challenging undertaking and both of you have to be willing and able to fight to make it work, even when you just don't feel like it. That means these qualities have to be part of his very nature and yours. But the bottom line is—if they aren't part of who he is now, chances are they never will be.

Love is friendship that has caught fire. It is quiet understanding, mutual confidence, sharing and forgiving. It is loyalty through good and bad times. It settles for less than perfection and makes allowances for human weaknesses.

ANN LANDERS

A Few Simple Tests

Given that many of these qualities are vague, it might be difficult to decide whether or not he measures up to your standards based on what you know about him today. It definitely takes lots of time and shared experiences to really know someone completely. There are a few tests you can do, however, to get a clearer picture of how he behaves. Use these methods to separate yourself from him and look at him more objectively.

The Inner-Circle Test

Study those people he surrounds himself with. We are all influenced by our friends to some degree. We usually pick them because they are like us in many ways. So pay attention to his friends, their behavior, and their values. Do they cheat on their girlfriends like crazy? If they do, he may think cheating is okay. Do they hold steady jobs and have goals? If so, he probably does too. Of course, there are instances in which he will differ from his friends, but you can get a general idea of what type of people influence him by watching the men he surrounds himself with. You have cause for alarm if:

- He spends most of his time with bachelors who think commitments are a burden.
- Many of his friends are involved in illegal activities like drug dealing or white-collar crime.
- He talks about how often his best friend cheats on his girlfriend as if there's nothing wrong with it.

- You notice his friends all think it's funny to degrade women and talk about them as if they are objects.
- Most of his buddies spend more than they can afford on expensive "toys" like fancy cars, yachts, and elaborate electronics. The guys all compete with each other and show off their goods.

The Role-Model Test

Pay close attention to his family and what they value. Are his parents still married? Does his father cheat and lie, or is he an honest man? Are his parents responsible? While he will certainly not be exactly like them, he will have adopted at least some of their views. It's important that he has some positive role model in his life like an older couple he knows well who have been in a committed relationship for a long time. It doesn't have to be his parents, but it has to be someone he respects, so he believes they know what they are doing and he is influenced to live his life in a similar way. You have cause for alarm if:

- Most of the people in his family are divorced, including his parents, his siblings, his aunts and uncles. He shows no signs that he's committed to breaking this family tradition.
- He puts his father on a pedestal even though his dad is an extremely angry or negative person.
- All of his siblings have gone astray; they don't hold steady jobs or have any responsibilities.
- He doesn't have any older people in his life who live their lives the way you want to live yours.

- He has a bad relationship with everyone in his family even though you've met them and they seem like nice, genuine people.

The Job Test

What type of profession has your guy picked and what are the people in that profession usually like? Is he a corporate lawyer who feels pressure to work long hours? Is he an investment banker who values making money above all else? Does he work in construction and spend the off-season hanging out with the guys? Is he a prosecutor who is in danger sometimes because of the criminals he puts away?

While there are exceptions to the rule in every profession, the job a man chooses does say something about his values, his ambition level, and what he wants his future to be like. His job will be a major part of his life, and yours too. Can you live with it? He might not be the right guy for you if:

- His office culture is one of chauvinism and arrogance and it seems to be influencing him.
- His coworkers all cheat on their wives and cheat at work too. He hangs out with them and looks up to them.
- He's an investment professional, so his sole purpose is to make money, and you don't want the pursuit of money to be a major part of your life.
- He's in a creative profession where most people live a bohemian lifestyle and you want more structure in your life.
- He's a cop, a fireman, or in the armed forces and you're not sure you can live with the level of danger in his career.

The "Just a Friend" Test

Imagine a female friend of yours taking on all the qualities and values of your guy. Would you still be friends with her? Is she someone you would want to spend time with? Sometimes we evaluate a person differently when we're dating them than we would if that person were just a friend. We tend to ignore faults and make excuses for bad behavior when we're in a romantic relationship. So try to separate his values and actions from him by imagining what he would be like as a female friend and how you would feel about him then. You have cause for alarm if:

- You used to have a friend just like him and you stopped hanging out with her because she wasn't a nice person.
- You notice that when you think about one of your girlfriends acting the way he acts, it makes you cringe.
- You realize you are overlooking many bad qualities simply because you are attracted to him.
- You know if you dragged him along to girls' night out dressed as a woman, your other girlfriends wouldn't want to hang out with him.

The Movie Test

Imagine your guy is a character in a movie. Do you side with him or think he's a jerk? Do you want to see him win at the end? If you were asked to write a screenplay based on his life, how would you portray him and how would other people react to his character? Once again, this exercise is simply a way to remove yourself from the equation and look at the way he lives his life objectively. You need to feel like you want to see your guy win. Romance aside, do you want to see him succeed? Are you cheering for him? You have cause for alarm if:

- The name of the screenplay would be *The Modern-Day Psycho.*
- You would have to cast yourself as his miserable sidekick.
- You're hoping the aliens will eat him alive.
- You can't figure out a way to make him likable to the audience.
- It will be a happy ending only if he doesn't survive the last major attack scene.

The Story-Telling Test

What types of stories does he tell you about his past? Pay close attention to them. These stories say something about what he values. They indicate what he's proud of in his life and what he wants to showcase. So if he tells you he gets ahead because he's a skilled liar, he probably thinks you are going to be impressed by his skills. If he tells you his biggest accomplishment in life was finally learning how to cheat on his taxes, you can glean that he doesn't value honesty. Also, pay attention to what he tells you about his exes, how he broke up with them, and what they think of him now. Does he still get nasty letters from them or do they leave him alone? Are they in therapy now or do they still speak highly of him? While he might embellish stories trying to impress you, what he chooses as the topic matter can tell you a lot about who he is and what is important to him. You have cause for alarm if:

- He never tells you a single story about his past. In fact, he seems to be hiding something.
- All of his favorite stories involve him shooting animals or beating up his brother.
- He gets hate mail from ex-girlfriends regularly.
- A Google search brings up information about the restraining order one of his exes took out against him.
- His stories about his life don't match those his parents tell you in any way.

Back to You

So, do you think he treats other people well even when he's not with you? Does he seem like a genuinely good guy? If the answer is "no," it's time to let him go. But if the answer is "yes," you can now assess how he displays these qualities when he's with you. If you've evaluated him accurately up to this point, and determined that he's a great guy, it should be very easy to see that he's also a great guy when he's by your side. Think about those ways in which he demonstrates to you that he's a good person.

Does He Show You That He Cares about You?

Does he do special little things for you to make you happy? Does he call and ask you if you want something when he's at the store? Does he make you dinner sometimes or bring you soup when you're sick? He might seem like the most caring person in the world when you first meet him because he's trying to impress you, but eventually he won't have the same energy he had at first. He might slack off on the cute little gestures, send flowers less often, and forget to bring you home orange juice when you ask him to do so. Nevertheless, if you've determined that he's generally a caring person, this quality will always be present in your relationship somehow.

Does He Support You?

Does he get on the phone and argue with the customer service representative for you if your new purchase isn't working properly? Does he tell you how proud he is of you when you get a big fat raise? Do you feel like he's on your side? Of course he'll do things sometimes that are anything but supportive. He might freak out about your raise because you're making more money than he is. He might tell you that you're wrong when you get into a fight with your sister. But if he's a supportive person most of the time, you'll feel like he's on your side and you won't want to dump him for those little instances when he's not.

Is He Honest with You?

Has he ever lied to you in a significant way about where he is, what he's doing, and who he's with? Do you trust that he's telling you the truth about what he does when he's out with his friends? It might not be a big deal if he tells you he had only two drinks and he had four or if he tells you he got home at 1:00 A.M. and he arrived at 2. Everyone tells these little fibs just to make the person they love feel a little more at ease. If you know he values honesty in other people, you can be certain when it comes to the big issues that really matter, he will always tell the truth.

Is He Loyal to You?

Has he ever cheated on you? Does he flirt behind your back? Has he told his friends secrets that you didn't want him to divulge or talked negatively about you to them? If you know he's done any of these things, you can't trust him because he's not loyal to you. However, sometimes it's difficult to know for sure whether or not someone is being completely loyal in a relationship. Obviously, you aren't there to watch him all the time. So you have to trust blindly. You will be able to do so if you know he values loyalty in others and he's consistently loyal to his friends, his family, and his values.

Is He Responsible in Your Relationship?

Does he show up for dates when he says he's going to or does he stand you up? Does he run errands for you when you ask him to? Can you trust him to pay you back when you loan him money or to mail an important document for you? Does he take responsibility for his actions when he hurts your feelings? Surely, he'll fail to do something you ask him to do at some point, or he'll act in an irresponsible manner and hurt your feelings, but if he's usually a responsible person, these little slip ups won't bother you enough to cause the whole relationship to come crashing down.

Does He Have Patience with You?

Does he yell at you when you're taking too long to get ready? Does he snap at you if you bug him while he's watching television? Does he talk to you calmly or get anxious when you're trying to have a serious discussion? Is he always fidgeting when you're trying to get him to pay attention to something you're saying? Most of us have moments where we lack patience with the person we love either because we're in a bad mood or because they've said something to push us over the edge. If he's a patient person most of the time, however, you will be able to handle with ease the little instances when he's not.

Is He Brave When It Comes to Matters That Affect You?

Does he reveal his feelings to you even though he's scared to? Is he brave enough to admit to you when he's wrong? Does he step up and fight with the car dealer when the guy is trying to jip you? Certainly, he may run away screaming when he sees a bug, or hide under a blanket during a scary movie, but if he values bravery, he will act courageously when it matters most.

> A hero is no braver than an ordinary man, but he is brave five minutes longer.
>
> RALPH WALDO EMERSON

Is He Unselfish in the Relationship?

Does he drink all the coffee in the morning even though he knows you want a cup? Does he offer you a bite of his sandwich or eat the whole thing right in front of you? Of course he'll have moments when he's acting pretty selfish, when his childlike instincts take over and he demands his own way. But you won't feel too alarmed by these moments if you've witnessed him acting unselfishly on numerous other occasions.

It's extremely important that the guy you're dating demonstrates these noble qualities when he is with you, but it's equally important that they are part of who he is at the core. Though scientists can't agree on whether personality is a result of nature (genetic influences) or nurture (environmental influences), they all agree that it's tough to change someone's personality when he or she is an adult. So what you see is what you get. And when you're trying to decide if a man is right for you, this fact is one you should take very seriously. If you don't like what you see right now, do not invest any more energy and time into the relationship.

chapter seven

The Single Self

Being part of a couple is kind of like taking up a new sport. At first, it's demanding because you're learning all of the rules of the game. But after you've practiced for a while, the role of girlfriend becomes second-nature. The relationship turns into a fun, familiar part of your life and the days really start to whiz by.

But one day you wake up, a year or two down the road, and you notice that your life has changed. You see for the first time that there's distance between your world now and the world you knew as a single woman. You realize that by being part of this relationship, you've lost touch with parts of your single self . . . and you miss them.

When we sense that our relationship might move to a more serious level, we have complex feelings about leaving our single life behind. We're excited, but we're scared. We want someone to rely on, but we don't want to lose the independent person that we are. We look forward to being a fiancé or a wife, but we want to define these roles our own way.

When you have these complicated feelings, you might wonder if maybe it has something to do with your guy. "Perhaps he's not right," you think. "Maybe if he was, I would be ready to take the plunge wholeheartedly and none of these issues would bother me." But it's normal to feel confused during this transitional time. Whenever we move to a new phase in our lives, we feel excited and a little bit scared. Just remember that you don't have to choose between "me" and "we." You're not replacing the person that you were. You're building on it. And if the relationship is right for you, you will be able to maintain those parts of your single self that you cherish most while welcoming the new dimension he brings to your life.

Out of the Comfort Zone

We spend so much time when we're single thinking and talking about becoming part of a twosome. Even though we're busy with a career and friends, most of us hope to meet a great guy at some point, not because we need one but because we're excited about what he will add to our lives. It never crosses our mind that we might actually have second thoughts about being in a relationship once we're there. But as modern women, we spend the early part of our lives becoming self-sufficient and learning to be happy on our own. So naturally we feel a little bit apprehensive when we have to fit another person into the world we've created.

Our Fears

Some of your fears might be absurd, worst-case scenarios like, "What if he has a hundred thousand dollars in credit card debt he's not telling me about?" or "What if I Google him one day and find out he's wanted for drug trafficking in another country?" We've all read some unbelievable news story about a seemingly normal boyfriend gone bad and worried that it might happen to us. But you probably have some very rational fears as well, and those are the ones you should focus on here. What scares you about committing to your guy? Are these fears caused by something he is doing or are you simply afraid of moving out of your comfort zone and into a place that is a little less familiar?

Fear #1: Losing Your Independence

When you were single, you had mastered the art of being happy—alone. In fact, you really enjoyed your freedom, flirting, hanging out with friends, and doing your own thing. But you had to pay a price for this independence. You had to recover from tough breakups, move a few times, and take risks in your career to finally get to this place of total self-reliance. Even now that you've been dating your guy for a while, you still go out with your friends and go on trips without him sometimes. But you wonder, "Will I still be able to do these things if the relationship gets even more serious? Will I have to give up my independence if we get engaged or married?" These thoughts are incredibly scary for any woman who is used to being on her own. But keep in mind that chances are, you will have fears like these regardless of who you're dating.

When you begin to think about making a commitment to someone, the potential sacrifices involved become a lot more real. Your fears are not a sign that this particular guy is wrong, unless:

- You feel like he's taking over parts of your life without your consent. Perhaps he answers for you when someone asks you a question or he insists on ordering for you when you're out to dinner.
- He doesn't respect you for having an independent streak. He criticizes you for having your own opinions and goals.
- He complains that you don't need him and he wants you to prove to him that you do by giving up things that are important to you.
- He's demanding that you move to a place you don't want to move to, where you will be cut off completely from the life you love now.
- You decide you just don't want a relationship and that the whole notion of fusing your life with another person's is not for you.

Fear #2: Having Less Time for Other People

Sometimes when you're having a nice quiet dinner with your guy, you remember days long ago when you went out every night to rowdy bars with your girlfriends and lived it up. Sometimes you stumble upon an old picture and feel nostalgic about the fun times you had. But things have changed and life seems to be even busier now than it used to be. You work, go to the gym, and have a million other things going on, so you spend most of your free time with him. You even see your family less now. You miss these other people but you also don't need them as much as you used to and that makes you kind of sad.

When you sense that your guy is becoming your "family" and those people who once played that role are no longer first in your life, it will make you feel sad. You might even feel like you're betraying your single friends, or your parents, by making your guy a priority. These feelings are very normal. They are a problem only if:

- He's preventing you from seeing your family and friends. He's doing things to isolate you from contact with the outside world.
- You feel like he's unfairly monopolizing your time. He's needy and requires constant attention to be happy.
- He hates your family or your friends and refuses to make any effort to get along with them.
- He can't understand why you need to have a night out with the girls on occasion.

The way to love anything is to realize that it may be lost.

GILBERT K. CHESTERTON

Fear #3: Losing Your Space and Privacy

You have your own apartment or house, or maybe it's just a dorm room, but it's yours. You have it arranged your way. You have your own closet space, your own bathroom, and all the privacy in the world. At first, you enjoyed "playing house." He would come over and cook you dinner or you would do his laundry. You didn't mind sharing your space with your guy, but that's because you knew you could always tell him to leave. Now you wonder, "What will life be like if he is around *all* the time? He's so messy and he never cleans. How will I deal with his dirty ways? He has ugly furniture and thousands of trinkets and trophies from high school. How can I tell him to leave those babies in storage?"

When you're used to doing things your way, on your terms, a guy encroaching on your space might bring back traumatic teenage memories of your sister snooping through your stuff. But you can learn to live with another person again and it will never be as bad as having your snoopy sister lingering nearby. This fear of losing your privacy and space is a problem only if:

- He doesn't show any respect for you, your space, or your things. He comes over, sets his dirty shoes on your kitchen table and rubs his smelly feet on your new white couch.
- He insists that the place you live together will be decorated *his* way because you don't know the first thing about design.
- He "accidentally" finds your diaries while you're at the store, reads them, and then yells at you about the contents.
- He insists on prominently displaying a sentimental item that his ex-girlfriend gave him.
- He insists on bringing with him guns, strange sex toys, a marijuana plant, or anything else you don't want around when he moves in with you.

Fear #4: Missing Opportunities

You've worked hard to excel in your career. Perhaps you have earned a professional degree or you've worked your way up from assistant to a management position. You're proud of all you've accomplished and you have more you want to do. When a guy comes along and the two of you get serious, the relationship starts to limit your flexibility and time at work, and this can make you feel anxious. You don't want to stay late every night like you used to, but you don't want to slack off, either. You can't accept a better job offer in another state because you have someone else to consider. And you can see that this balancing act is only going to get harder. Eventually you'll have to figure out how to balance your personal goals and your career with a family. The notion of doing it all seems impossible. All successful, driven women worry about these issues. It's not a sign that something is wrong with the guy you're with unless:

- He insists that his career comes first . . . period.
- You can't agree on who is going to do what if you have kids.
- After thinking about the relationship, you decide that you really don't care about him enough to compromise any part of your career, ever.
- He downplays the things you accomplish on your own and makes light of your job as if it's not really important.
- The two of you are viciously competitive with one another and always trying to outdo each other.

Fear #5: Growing Up

When you were single, you did something different each weekend for fun and that seemed to slow life down. Time didn't fly by like it does now that you're in a comfortable routine. You look back at the days gone by and wonder where the time went. And you notice that you feel much more like an adult now that you have a significant other. You used to think getting engaged or married was something older people do, but now you can sort of see yourself doing these things too.

Making a commitment to spend your life with another person is one of the most visible signs of the passage of time. Suddenly you are taking on a role that your parents always played. They become the older generation and you take their place. This process provokes strong feelings of fear and nostalgia in all of us. It's the wistfulness that comes with growing up, a feeling similar to the one we have when we graduate

memory triggers

Complex feelings about leaving the past behind can pop up at different times for different reasons. So don't be surprised if they are triggered by a variety of experiences like:

- Finding an old photograph of you and your friends
- Hearing a song that reminds you of the time before you met him
- Being asked by your mother or father just how serious you are about the relationship
- Attending someone else's wedding
- Reading through old e-mails or cards you've saved
- Finding out a friend's life is changing in a significant way
- Running into an ex or an old friend
- Ring shopping
- Bringing him back to your old neighborhood
- Seeing pictures of your parents when they first got married

from school or move away from home. Don't be surprised if you have a hard time letting go of the past and all it represents. Just realize that these feelings are normal, and they don't have anything to do with your guy unless:

- You are certain that if he becomes a permanent part of your life, the future won't be all that you want it to be.
- You look back at days gone by and realize that you were very happy then and now you are miserable.
- You think your desire to live a young, carefree life is going to cause you to be unfaithful to your guy at some point.
- You realize that you're too young to be in the relationship and you haven't lived enough to be sure it's what you want. You truly aren't ready to grow up yet.

Torn in Two

It can be very difficult to separate your feelings for your guy from your feelings about the changes and challenges he represents. Nevertheless, recognize that many, if not all, women go through this complicated period of adjustment, and it is, in part, a product of the time in which we live.

Marriage today just isn't necessary like it used to be years ago. We don't need a man for economic support, protection, or even to have children. So the decision to be with him is truly a decision we undertake freely, or so we think.

Interestingly, whereas women once felt pressure to get married, today sometimes we feel pressure not to commit to a guy. We're told to wait and build our own life first. But many women, regardless of their age, location, and social circles, confirm that both of these conflicting currents exist in our culture—pressure to marry and pressure not to. So you might think that you can't make up your mind about your guy because you are picky or you just aren't a decisive person or he isn't quite right, when in reality you are receiving confusing signals from the world around you. This phenomenon can make you unsure of your relationship and what role you want a guy to play in your life. You might feel as if you must:

- Respect and rely on a man, yet cherish your independence
- Support and honor him, yet speak your mind and make your preferences known
- Play the dating game, yet be yourself
- Buy into tradition, yet embrace the future
- Marry someone who is like you, but encourage differences to keep life exciting
- Look beyond the superficial, yet have an eye toward his earning potential
- Work without being a bad mother and wife
- Stay at home without losing yourself and your goals
- Want a commitment and yet not want one so badly that it dominates your life

With all of these confusing signals coming our way, it's amazing that we ever make up our mind about what we want out of a relationship. Just remember that the decision truly is yours. Don't let complex and often contradictory cultural expectations of women cloud your true feelings, good or bad, for the man in your life.

Selective Memory

Regardless of how serious your relationship is, before you're engaged, it still has an air of impermanence. In the back of your mind, you know that you really haven't committed to anything yet. You still have an "out"—not that you would choose to take it, but it is there.

But a time might come when you seriously consider taking that "out." You feel so anxious about leaving your single world behind that you decide you just can't do it. You would rather go back to living life on your own, hanging out with friends, and being your own person without any attachments. But before you ditch your guy for the life you once knew, remember that it wasn't always as perfect as you remember it to be. We often romanticize the past and forget that it, too, had its own unique set of challenges. Being part of a relationship can be demanding and confusing, but living life on your own can be too, and that's an important fact to remember.

> Women today are dealing with both their independence and also the fact that their lives are built around finding and satisfying the romantic models we grew up with.
>
> JANE CAMPION

Celebrate the days gone by because they were, without a doubt, exciting and fulfilling, but remember that the past wasn't always as perfect as you remember it to be.

Memory: High school was a fun, carefree adventure when time was on your side and the world was full of possibility. Oh to be young again.

Reality: You battled acne; cliquey, annoying girls; and angst about the future. You always had homework hanging over your head and the SAT looming in the distance.

Memory: You had so much fun with your ex-boyfriend. The two of you would be entertained for hours just walking around the city and window shopping.

Reality: He used to drive you crazy when he would gawk at every woman on the street and the mannequins in the windows. Ultimately you were glad to see him go.

Memory: Nights out at dance clubs were so exhilarating. Nothing can compare to the feeling of being surrounded with great girlfriends and an open bar.

Reality: Sometimes you got really tired of being squeezed into a tiny space with sweaty arms brushing up against you.

Memory: It was so fun to talk to friends over coffee about all of the men you were dating and which ones you really liked.

Reality: At least half of the time you were stressing out about the way these guys were behaving and what the future would bring.

Memory: It was absolutely liberating to sign the lease for your very own apartment.

Reality: You also coughed up a huge check for the security deposit and felt sick when you handed it over to the realtor.

Memory: Having time to yourself every weekend was so much fun. You could just come home, take a bath, do your nails, and watch television.

Reality: Sometimes you were bored out of your mind and you would go for long walks just to have something to do.

Memory: Dating lots of guys was a blast. The future was so full of promise and that was exciting.

Reality: At times you thought you might die if you had to go on one more painful date.

Obviously, life as a single woman is an extraordinary experience full of excitement and possibility. It's a time when you get to pursue your own goals and needs without worrying about anybody else's. Nevertheless, it is important to remember that it was also difficult in many ways. Each phase of life introduces a new set of challenges.

Do not trust your memory; it is a net full of holes; the most beautiful prizes slip through it.

GEORGES DUHAMEL

Major Gains

When you choose to become part of a committed relationship, you aren't leaving behind a whole life you once new. You're gaining a new one. You're taking those things from your single life that you love and building on top of them new memories, new skills, and new experiences. If the guy you choose is right for you, he will welcome people from your past, stories you remember, and those parts of your personality that were defined during your single days. You won't feel like these important things are lost for good because you're sharing them with the person you love.

The Flip Side of Fear

As you start to work through many of life's challenges with your guy, you'll find that many of the things you feared you would lose—independence, career opportunity, privacy, friends—aren't really gone at all. In fact, now you get to choose whether or not you want to make them a priority, and you have new things that are important to you as well. You are still your single self in many ways, but you also have your girlfriend role and you appreciate both of these parts of your life for different reasons.

Independence with a Cushion

When you're part of a committed relationship, you can still do your own thing, speak your mind, and pay your own way anytime you wish. But now you have someone in your life to fall back on during those times when you just don't feel like being self-reliant. The right man is there for you when you need him, but he doesn't *make* you need him. You have the power to choose when to be your sassy self and when to reach out to him for support. And don't forget that you choose to be in the relationship and that choice is empowering in its own right. You are the one taking your life in the direction you want it to go.

New People

When you're part of a committed relationship, the people you once knew aren't gone. You can still make an effort to go out with friends, spend time with your family, and do all of the fun things you used to do. But you might find that in some cases, you just don't want to do the same things anymore. Just as we outgrow certain friends when we leave high school or college, we change what we're looking for in friends as we grow older. Some of your friends will stay with you throughout your life, and they will seem to fit regardless of whether you are single or dating, married or divorced, young or old, but others will not.

Being part of a serious relationship also brings new people into your life. You have his family, his friends, and those friends you meet as a couple. You really have more social options than you did as a single woman as long as you keep making an effort to stay in touch with people.

New Opportunities

When you're part of a committed relationship, you might have to forgo some of your late nights at the office, but you'll also have new opportunities to be successful in your life. You will have a relationship and family to work on, and success in these personal areas will be rewarding too. If he's the right guy for you, he will support the career choices you make and work with you to come up with alternative ways to achieve your goals if the old ways are no longer viable. Your relationship is a partnership, and you're there to help each other be happy and successful. You work to create new opportunities for one another, not to destroy them.

New Things to Share

When you're part of a committed relationship, you will still have personal space and privacy, but you'll have the option of giving it up when you want to. If he's the right guy for you, he'll respect your need for space sometimes. But there are also many parts of your life that you'll want to share with him. You'll welcome the chance to reveal some of your thoughts, opinions, and fears with someone you trust.

Relationships do require sacrifice and compromise. You do have to give things up sometimes when you have someone else's needs and happiness to consider. But you're not really losing anything because for every wonderful experience you leave behind, a new one will take its place.

> It's choice—not chance—that determines your destiny.
>
> JEAN NIDETCH

The Perils of Predicting

Sometimes anticipating a big change in your life can be a little bit like being an anxious kid on the last night of summer vacation. Remember? You knew your teacher's name but you didn't know who would be in your class or how the year would unfold. You lay in bed and imagined who you might *new rituals*   You might be glad to say goodbye to many of the rituals you had as a single woman, but you'll also welcome new girlfriend rituals. Things like:

OLD RITUAL: You used to eat an entire pint of ice cream while watching girly movies.
NEW RITUAL: You hide the ice cream behind the ice tray so he can't find it. Then you sneak bites of it while he's in the shower.

OLD RITUAL: You used to buy a special shampoo to use before you went on a date.
NEW RITUAL: You buy two shampoos—a high-quality one for you and a generic one for him because his hair just doesn't need the extra shine.

OLD RITUAL: You used to blast diva music and girly songs before you went out at night.
NEW RITUAL: You blast diva music and girly songs whenever you want him to leave the house for a while.

OLD RITUAL: You used to buy sexy pajamas in case your guy stayed over.
NEW RITUAL: You keep your collection of T-shirts and boxers updated so you never run out of bedtime wear.

OLD RITUAL: You used to shave your legs every day.
NEW RITUAL: You dry-shave them once a week because, heck, that's good enough.

sit next to or what it would be like to be one year older. And inevitably most of what you imagined never came to pass. The world you entered and the things you experienced that year were far different than those you dreamed about on that last night of summer.

Remember this lesson from your younger days and apply it to your life now. Whatever picture you're painting in your head of what life will be like in the years to come is inevitably a little different than the way it will really pan out. Many of the situations you fear will never come to pass, but you'll also face challenges that you can't anticipate. You might think you'll miss certain things about your old life and find you're relieved when they are gone.

Likewise, someday you might remember fondly things you don't recall right now. So the point is that you can't make a clear decision about your guy based on what-ifs and worries. You can only make the best decision you can based on the information you have today.

Achieving Balance

Finding a balance between "me" and "we" in a relationship is not always easy. But if this balance is important to both of you, you can find ways to do it. So your first step is to make sure that he's on board. Does he value his "single life" too? Does he view the relationship as a chance to fuse the new with the old? Does he see it as an opportunity to build a new life together in addition to, not in place of, the one you've both created as individuals? If you share these goals for your future, you will be able to reach them. To achieve balance in your life, remember to do the following:

- **CREATE YOUR OWN TRADITIONS.** You'll both bring with you your favorite customs and traditions. You don't have to choose between his way and yours. You can create new ways of doing things that bring together the best parts of both of your worlds.

- **CONTINUE TO PARTICIPATE IN YOUR OWN INDEPENDENT ACTIVITIES.** Your relationship will be stronger if you both maintain outside interests. Then, when you're together, you'll always have something new and interesting to talk about in addition to discussing your shared interests.

- **KEEP YOUR OWN FRIENDS IN YOUR LIFE.** If you expect him to fulfill all your needs all the time, you'll be let down. And you certainly can't fulfill all of his needs either. You both need to have many people in your lives. When he can't be a listening ear, a girlfriend will take his place. Likewise, when you can't understand his guy problems, he will have other guys to share them with.

- **CREATE PERSONAL ESCAPES.** You both need alone time, and if you neglect this need, you'll feel claustrophobic in the relationship. A personal escape doesn't have to be a place far away. It can be an activity like reading or time spent writing in your journal.

- **TALK TO EACH OTHER.** Nothing is more important than sharing your feelings and concerns with one another. When you discuss a problem together, you'll come up with new solutions you couldn't think of on your own. If you can't talk to each other openly about what's important to you, the relationship cannot survive.

women talk about change Women everywhere experience complex feelings when they are thinking about getting more serious with a guy. But many women who've already gone through this experience will confess that their fears were unfounded and they are happy they made the leap.

- "I used to have moments when I felt like I was missing something by not being out with my single friends. But at one point I realized that the world I knew when I was single didn't even exist anymore. We had all moved on."—*Keri, age 31*

- "I lost sleep on countless occasions worrying about how I would balance my career ambitions with a family. But it was easier than I thought it would be. When we had kids, my husband understood my anxieties and helped in every way. When we worked together, solutions popped up that we never even thought of."—*Mia, age 44*

- "I always thought it would be absolutely impossible to live with a guy, having him there all the time every day. But now that he does live with me, I feel like not seeing him enough has turned out to be the bigger problem."—*Noreen, age 32*

- "I felt very nervous about getting married, but by our one-year anniversary, I couldn't even remember what my life was like when I was single. It just seemed like he had always been a part of my world."—*Jessica, age 35*

- TALK TO OTHER PEOPLE WHO SHARE YOUR SITUATION.
  Remember to tell other women how you feel about leaving your
  single self behind and share with them your fears about the
  future. You'll be relieved to hear that they feel the same way you
  do. They will offer you a new perspective and ways to get past
  your anxieties and move forward.

It's normal to feel a little bit strange when you think about
making a real commitment to the guy in your life. You can't
help but wonder how your life will change and if you'll be
happy with the changes. But remember that you have control
over your future and you can make your relationship what you
want it to be. You don't have to say good-bye to everything that
was important to you when you were single. You can bring
many parts of that single self with you. And the right guy will
appreciate that side of you. He'll add a new dimension to the
life you already know.

chapter eight

The Right Fit

Once you've determined that your guy has important qualities like honesty, patience, and loyalty, and that he shares your interests, you're well on your way to declaring him worthy of your ring finger.

Nevertheless, as you look around, you probably know other guys who have these qualities too. So you have to ask, "What sets my guy apart from all of the rest?" Why him and not any other man out there who also fits these criteria? The answer is quite simple. He's the right fit for you.

What is "fit"? Some call it friendship and others call it a connection. It's an element that can be difficult to describe, but it doesn't have to be. After all, we've all experienced "fit" before. Think about shopping for jeans. Have you ever taken five pairs of perfectly stylish, cool jeans into the dressing room only to try them on and discover that none of them make you happy? But eventually—sometimes when you're not even looking for them—you find that one pair that simply looks and feels great. Put simply, that's the right fit. They don't cling to your body too tightly, and they don't hang too loosely. They complement you in every way.

Likewise, when a guy "fits" you well, you feel like he has something special that really makes you happy. That something special isn't always easy to put into words, but you can try. Think about guy shopping. Okay, so you don't really "shop" for guys, but think about the times when you've gone out on dates with a few different men and they were all perfectly nice, but for some reason you just didn't feel like they were right for you. The conversation was good and they seemed smart, but they needed something more. Then, you met your guy, and he made you laugh and feel comfortable. You felt like you could talk to him with ease, kind of like you feel when you meet a good friend for the first time. He was the right fit. Or maybe you didn't feel this way and he wasn't the right fit? Think about how you relate to one another when you're together and determine whether or not he really does fit you fabulously like he should.

A Favorite Pair

To determine whether or not your guy fits you well, think a little bit more about your favorite pair of jeans. What makes them your favorite? You feel good about who you are when you're wearing them, right? They aren't just a pair you pick for one particular night out—they work well for a variety of occasions. The same holds true for a guy who fits well. You aren't just with him right now to pass the time or to have a date for an important event. When life changes or you change, the right guy still gels with you. And the best part is that while your favorite jeans might wear out, your relationship with your favorite guy gets better with age. You have more than just a superficial connection. Consider these important elements of fit and assess whether or not your guy has them.

Fun and Happiness

Do you have fun with your guy? Does he make you laugh? Do you share the same sense of humor? Do you have fun together even when you're not doing anything particularly exciting, when you're both just sitting in a room reading magazines? Is there a certain banter or level of playfulness that permeates your interactions, one that makes you enjoy life together?

At some point you need to shove all the serious issues and questions aside and just ask yourself flat out, "Do I have a ball when I'm with this guy? Is dinner better with him sitting across from me because he talks about interesting things and knows how to make me laugh?" In some ways, these questions are totally superficial. But he has to be fun for you if you're going to spend your life with him. You have to look forward to seeing him and spending time with him if you're going to live in the same place together. In other words, is he at least as amusing as your favorite television show? Is he a step up from your dog? If not, why would you even consider spending your life with him? You have to have fun with this guy or he's not a good fit. You'll know he fits well on this level if:

- Your gut reaction to these questions is, "Of course he's fun! Yes, he makes me happy." You didn't even have to think about it for a second.
- You spend a lot of timing laughing when you're with him (not laughing at him).
- You look forward to seeing him most of the time. An evening is better, a drive is better, and life itself is better when he's with you.
- You spend less time complaining about your life to friends and family now that you're with him and more time telling them how fantastic he is.
- When you're waiting for him on a park bench, and he's walking toward you from far away, when his face first comes into view, it makes you smile.

The real test of friendship is: can you literally do nothing with the other person? Can you enjoy those moments of life that are utterly simple?

EUGENE KENNEDY

The Real You

Are you the *real* you when you're with your guy? In other words, can you open up and be yourself, show your sweet side and your whiny side, and be open about your opinions? Remember, we love our favorite pair of jeans because they fit us the way we are today. They make us comfortable. Your guy has to fit with you the way you are right now. You have to feel like he was made for you and you can be yourself around him. He's a good fit if:

- You feel comfortable telling him your opinion on a political issue even if you know he won't agree with it.
- He doesn't really care what you wear as long as you feel good in it.
- He appreciates the quirky things about you that make you unique, like the way you sing Sinatra songs when you're in the shower or the way you dance while putting dishes in the dishwasher.
- You can cry when you want to cry, eat when you want to eat, and sleep when you want to sleep. You don't feel pressure from him to act a certain way.

Enhancing Your Assets

When you enter a relationship, you should already feel good about yourself and your life. You shouldn't be looking to him to fulfill you or make you more confident. However, he should still enhance the assets that you've already built on your own, just like a good pair of jeans makes your great body look even better.

Does he bring out your good side? Do you make each other stronger, more complete people? He should:

- Give you that little boost of encouragement when you're feeling down
- Make you so happy that you feel like being nicer and more patient with everyone around you
- Give you newfound energy to pursue your goals

- Give you new opportunities to show your loving, caring side
- Pick up the slack where you fall short; for example, be the voice of reason if you're an impulsive shopper
- Point out your strengths and remind you they are there when you forget about them

> Perhaps the feelings that we experience when we are in love represent a normal state. Being in love shows a person who he should be.
>
> ANTON CHEKHOV

The Little Things

Your favorite pair of jeans might have cool stitching or be just the right shade of blue. They might be ripped a certain way or have unique embroidery on the pockets. Your guy should also have little things about him that you love. These habits or traits might not be noticeable to anyone else in the world. Can you think of unique things about him that you find adorable or funny, things that another guy could never replicate? They might include the following:

- He'll only drink strawberry margaritas when you're together and he makes you pinky swear not to tell his guy friends.
- He insists on humming "Vogue" and pretending he's on a runway every time he tries on a new shirt.
- He pouts his lips like a baby to get his own way—it makes your heart melt.

- He has a unique ability to put life's problems in perspective.
- He loves to spoon with your cat.
- He's been known to dance around with your bra on his head just for attention.
- He does hysterical impersonations of everyone you know.

When a guy fits well, you are happy when you're with him. He enhances your life. That's not to say that you never have arguments or problems. Of course you do. But most of the time, when you're with him, life is just a bit better. And while you can point to qualities that he has that you admire, when it comes down to it, there are a thousand little things that you like about him that don't fit neatly into any specific category. They aren't things you'll find listed as "signs he's Mr. Right." They are his unique habits and traits that you notice and adore.

At different stages in our lives, the signs of love may vary: dependence, attraction, contentment, worry, loyalty, grief, but at heart the source is always the same. Human beings have the rare capacity to connect with each other, against all odds.

MICHAEL DORRIS

Forcing Him to Fit

Does your guy really fit or are you trying to force him to? Think again about your favorite pair of jeans from long ago, the ones you outgrew. At first you didn't want to get rid of them, so you would lie on the bed, suck in your stomach, and pull up the zipper. Then, you would do all sorts of stretches trying to get them to loosen up a little. Or maybe you tried to lose five pounds and change yourself to make them fit. But in the end, you had to donate them or sell them at a garage sale.

Likewise, if you're trying to make your guy fit, you'll find that you just can't. All you can do is slap a "5 cents" sticker on him and get rid of him at this year's yard sale. You can improve the relationship temporarily by putting extra effort into it, but it's almost impossible to make lasting changes. "Fit" is a natural bond between the two of you, not one you can create artificially. Think about those ways in which you might be trying to force him to fit.

> All love that has not friendship for its base is like a mansion built upon sand.
>
> ELLA WHEELER WILCOX

Signs of Struggle

Do you read about loving relationships and hone in on similarities to your situation while ignoring the stark differences? Do you overlook the bad things about the guy you're with and play up the good things? Here are a few signs that you are trying to make your square guy fit into a round hole:

- You spend excessive amounts of time trying to convince your family and friends that he's right for you.

defining "fit" While "fit" is difficult to define in a precise manner, many women in happy relationships recognize that they do feel it with the guy they're with. Here are some of the things they say are signs of the right fit:

- "I was dating my ex for about two months when he had a bunch of people over to his house for a party. I ended up hanging out in the kitchen all night talking to his friend about everything in the world. I knew at that point that my ex couldn't possibly be the right guy for me. I couldn't talk to him the way I could talk to his friend."—*Alyssa, age 32*

- "My boyfriend is the first person I call when something exciting happens, and the first person I talk to when I'm upset. I still have my friends around of course, and their support is important to me, but I enjoy sharing my life with my boyfriend. I feel like he really understands me." —*Stacy, age 27*

- "My husband and I notice the same subtleties in our environment. If someone is wearing a weird outfit or has a strange haircut, we both notice it. We agree on what's odd and what's funny."—*Joanne, age 38*

- "When I meet people, I always know quickly whether or not I like them. I wasn't sure that Mike was "The One" the first time we met, but I did know that he would be a good friend. As time progressed, I realized that we naturally fit together and the relationship felt right."—*Amy, age 33*

- You are working hard to get him to change the way he dresses, acts, or speaks.
- You like being with him when the two of you are alone, but you're embarrassed of him when you're with friends or coworkers.
- You're already attending couples counseling to work out your differences.
- You read relationship books and skip over the pages that contain information that might force you to conclude that he's not right for you.
- You are changing yourself, your look, your views, or your goals to make him like you more.
- Whenever you hear about someone else's horrible relationship, you immediately feel relieved because yours isn't *that* bad.
- Your head hurts from analyzing the relationship and rationalizing why you're still with him.

In every relationship, there are days when two people just don't fit together very well. If you have a day here or there where you're tired of each other or you just don't find his jokes funny, it is certainly no big deal. But if you feel that way most of the time, he's not the right guy for you. It simply can't last if he's not the right fit.

The 80 Percent Rule

You might feel at times like you don't fit in well with his family, his friends, or other people or circumstances related to him. Perhaps you don't feel comfortable with his siblings or you don't like the way he decorates his apartment. You might think, "Well, I fit with him, but what about all these other elements in his life that aren't such a good fit? Don't I have to fit with them too?" When this question arises, use the 80 percent rule to answer it. In other words, if you are having a problem with something in his life that will affect you over 80 percent of the time, it's an important issue to address. If it will affect you only once in a while, it's no big deal at all. For example:

He refuses to stray from the multicolored Picasso wall décor even though it makes his apartment look like a children's museum.
80 percent rule says: This issue will affect you all the time if you move in together. So either you have to learn to live with his preferences, or he has to tone down his artsy ways.

You really can't stand his mother. She criticizes you and offers unsolicited advice.
80 percent rule says: If she lives down the street, you will see her well over 80 percent of the time. So you need to address this issue with him and work out a way to put distance between the two of you and her. If you see her only two or three times a year, grin and bear it.

He loves to eat steak and you are a vegetarian. You wish more than anything that he would lay off the red meat.
80 percent rule says: Clearly his preference will affect you most of the time if you end up with this guy. You have to learn to come up with entrees that appeal to you both, agree to disagree, or talk him into having hamburger night with his buddies when you're not there.

His brother loves to crash on his couch, and half the time, he doesn't have any money, so he eats everything in the fridge.
80 percent rule says: If his brother lives nearby and there are no signs this behavior is going to stop, talk to your guy about it. If, however, he's just home for a few weeks before he moves across the country, let him crash until his heart's content.

Some of his friends are like animals. They love to drink excessively, they are all single, and you can't relate to them.
80 percent rule says: You're dating him, not his friends. As long as they aren't spending every waking moment at his place, they shouldn't be a problem in your relationship. You can learn to take his caveman buddies in small doses and be thankful he is the saner, more responsible member of the bunch.
You don't have to feel like you fit in perfectly with his family and friends. You only have to fit together well with your guy. So don't waste energy worrying about how you feel around them. Focus on making sure you fit well with him and that you can discuss openly any differences you have.

Breakup Barriers

Some women are bound to a guy by certain issues, experiences, or circumstances, so they work hard to make the guy fit even though he doesn't. Perhaps he helped them through the death of a parent or gave them support when they were sick. Sometimes he is the right fit and these experiences solidify the relationship. But often he's not, and the woman's feelings are clouded by these other issues. Does this sound like you?

a note on future in-laws

If you feel like you don't fit in with his family completely, don't worry. It's normal. They aren't your family so you should expect to feel a little out of place once in a while. If you notice they are sizing you up, remember that they are simply trying to make sure that you are good enough for their sweet angel boy. (In case you were wondering what that blood sample was for.) Don't be surprised if a few strange things happen when you're with them, like:

- You tell a joke about a weird African Congo disease and find out his grandmother just died from it.
- You can't decide if you should help his mother in the kitchen or simply go hide in a storage cabinet in the basement.
- You drop an heirloom dish on your way to the dining room.
- You ask his sister about something harmless—love life, education—only to find out that they "don't talk about those things."
- You bring them chocolate and they are all allergic to it.
- They pray before dinner and it feels a little strange for you.

Read through these common breakup barriers. If one of them pertains to you, dig deeper into your feelings to decide if he's really the right fit for you or you're just kidding yourself.

Family Ties

Does your mother adore him so much that you're terrified she'll disown you if you dump him? Are your parents adamant that you marry someone Jewish and he fits the profile? Pressure from family can hold two people together even when they aren't a good fit. The pressure might be obvious—your sisters won't stop talking about how perfect he is—or it might be subtle—your father invited him on his fishing trip. Obviously, family approval is not enough to hold two people together for life. Family pressures might be getting the best of you if:

- Your parents subtly suggest that you "hold on to him because he's [insert religion or cultural background]."
- Your mother cries when the two of you fight and yells at you for being too difficult.
- You have nightmares about telling family and friends that the two of you split.
- Your family has pushed you away from other men in the past that didn't fit their criteria.
- Your mother is already planning your big Italian wedding and you've only been dating him a few months.

Financial Circumstances

Are the two of you dependent on each other to pay the bills and take care of a household? Do you live together and rely on each other for economic support? Financial pressures are very real and sometimes difficult to overcome, but if they are the only bond between you, you will never feel like he fits with you the way you want him to. That means, as difficult as it may be, that you have to make an effort to break things off with him and make it on your own.

You are sticking with him due to financial pressures if:

- The first thought in your head when you think about breaking it off is, "Where would I live? How would I make my car payments?"
- You've made an effort to break up with him before but you keep coming back to him because you need the support.
- You pay his way and you don't have the heart to kick him out in the cold.
- You don't know how you'll make it through school if you don't have him around to help pay the rent.
- You don't want to give up the fancy lifestyle he provides.

Fear

Did you open up to him about your innermost feelings and now you're terrified he'll make fun of you to other people if you break up with him? Or has he threatened you and said scary things to you, like "If you break up with me, I'll kill you." You cannot have a fulfilling relationship based on terror tactics. Any type of threat qualifies as abuse, and you must report it to the police. If he's threatening you, not only is your relationship at risk, but your life is at risk. You are in the relationship because of fear if:

- You told him a deep, dark secret about your life and now you're afraid he's going to tell your friends if you break up with him.
- He has threatened to hurt himself, you, or your family if you leave him.

- He has harassed other ex-girlfriends or still does.
- He generally has an explosive personality and though he hasn't threatened you directly, you're scared of him.

Obligation

Did the two of you vow to one another that you'd never part, and now, as time goes by, you realize that you just don't belong together? People often stay in relationships because they feel obligated. They are afraid to hurt the other person or they feel like they are a hypocrite for saying "I love you" and then later breaking things off. Obviously, a relationship based on obligation doesn't have a future. You might be staying with him out of obligation if:

- You can't break up with him because he tells you every day how much he loves you.
- He proposed to you unexpectedly and you didn't know how to say no, so you just figured "this must be it" and you said yes.
- He expresses how much he cares about you to the entire world all the time and you feel like you're going to publicly humiliate him if you break up with him.
- You promised him you would help him pass the bar exam or get through his residency and now you feel like you need to fulfill that promise.

Nothing is a waste of time if you use the experience wisely.

AUGUSTE RODIN

A Big Move

Did the two of you go through college together, graduate, and move to the same city? Or did you buy a house together? Maybe you both decided on a whim to pick up and move across the country? When you invest the time and energy to make a big move together, it creates a bond between you that is tough to break. You might not know anyone else in the new city where you live, or you might share financial responsibility for an apartment. Obviously, this type of bond alone is not enough to sustain a relationship. So if it's the only thing holding you together, it's time to call it quits.

Disease or Death of a Loved One

Did he help you through the death of a family member or was he there for you through your own illness? Have you been there for him through a tragic circumstance in his life? These types of tough experiences create a very strong bond between two people. During a difficult time, you reveal your most vulnerable side to each other, and it brings you together. But when the experience is over, the comfort, care, and support you gave each other are not enough to sustain a relationship forever. You have to fit together in other ways too. You have to have fun together, laugh together, and feel like the relationship is right on a number of levels.

It's common to feel confused about your feelings for a guy if any of these factors are holding you together. These issues and experiences serve as "breakup barriers." They keep you

little tests

Is he the right fit? Ask yourself these questions:

- If my sister or best friend was in this relationship, what would I tell her to do?
- If I moved to a new city with him and no one else was there— no people, no family, no job—would his behavior or ways make me happy or would I feel alone?
- If I presented the facts to a jury of impartial people, would they decide I should stay with him or move on?
- Would I still love him if he lost all his hair? Or do I long to rip it out with a piece of duct tape?

hanging on even though you know deep inside that you should let go. Other, less significant barriers can also make women stay with a guy longer than they should—an astrologer or psychic says he's "The One" or he has a great last name or a holiday is coming up and you don't want to be alone for it. The bottom line is, any one of these issues is not reason enough to stay with your guy. There has to be something more if you want to sustain a long-term relationship. You have to have a special fit that makes you both happy to be together.

Settling Versus Questioning

To most discerning women, settling for the wrong guy is about as appealing as spending an evening at a monster truck rally when you really want to be at the Chanel runway after-party.

Are you settling in your relationship? Are you accepting something in spite of the fact that you are not completely satisfied with it? If you know in your heart that your guy is not a good fit for you but you choose to commit to him anyway, you're settling. If you are giving up a nonnegotiable, one of those critical qualities you know you need, you are settling.

But he doesn't have to be perfect in every way. The goal is to be satisfied, not overindulged. In other words, you don't have to be happy with your guy all the time, just most of the time. You need to feel content that in the areas that are most important to you, he measures up to your standards.

> It takes a lot of courage to release the familiar and seemingly secure, to embrace the new. But there is no real security in what is no longer meaningful. There is more security in the adventurous and exciting, for in movement there is life, and in change there is power.
>
> ALAN COHEN

It's very normal to ask questions before you commit to someone, and questioning is not the same thing as settling. You wouldn't buy an apartment or house without asking questions and hiring inspectors to look over your purchase. You wouldn't buy a car without finding out if it has all the features you're looking for. When you have questions about your guy, there are open issues that the two of you need to debate and discuss. When you settle, the answer is definitive and you don't like it, but you choose to ignore it. Make sure you understand the difference between settling and questioning.

Questioning: At times, you don't find him physically attractive but at other times you do. You wonder if he's really cute enough for you.

Settling: You do not find him attractive at all, but he makes a lot of money, so you're game to give it a try.

Questioning: Sometimes he's so into his work that you wonder if he'll make time for his family down the road.

Settling: He told you that he doesn't want a family and that his work comes first. You commit to him anyway and try to ignore this glaring difference in your life plans.

Questioning: He's lazy about taking care of household tasks and you have to nag him sometimes to get him to wash the dishes. You wonder if you can live with it.

Settling: He's lazy about everything and you can't stand it, but you commit anyway because you're afraid you won't meet anyone better.

Questioning: He checks out other women and sometimes it hurts your feelings. You wonder if it will stop if you talk to him about it.

Settling: He's cheated on you and made it clear that it's his right to check out other women. You convince yourself that that's the way all men are, so you commit to him anyway.

Questioning: You are strictly religious and he is a little more progressive in his faith. You wonder if these differences are going to be an issue at some point in the relationship.

Settling: He makes fun of your religious beliefs even though they are important to you. You decide that you'll just practice on your own and try not to bother him with anything spiritual.

When you question your guy, you know there are certain things about him that aren't perfect. You ask yourself, "Can I accept this difference between us? Is he right for me?" You explore the answers and you decide whether you can live with them or not. When you settle, you already know the answers and you don't like them, but you decide to commit to him anyway. You accept the fact that he's not the right fit, and you resign yourself to a life that's not what you want it to be.

Obviously, it's important not to settle for a guy who isn't right for you. So use the guidelines in this chapter to determine whether or not your guy is the right fit. Does he make you happy? Does he make your life better? These questions might seem obvious, but plenty of women live for years with men who don't add any value to their lives. Don't allow yourself to be one of these women. Assess your guy objectively and make sure he's the right fit before you move forward.

chapter nine

The Committing Kind

By now you've probably figured out that deciding if a guy is right for you is no easy task. You can arrive at this decision only after asking and answering the right questions and sorting through your complex feelings about his place in your life. If, after going through this process, you've decided that you do think he is the guy for you, commitment might be the next thing on your mind. But what does commitment really mean? Though you are probably committed to each other to some extent already—you're in an exclusive relationship and you've pledged your love—this chapter will focus on "commitment" in the more formal sense of the word: engagement.

Your formal, public commitment to each other begins the moment you get engaged. Many of us, guys and girls alike, are excited about the idea of getting engaged, but we don't really understand what it means. We focus on the tangible elements—a proposal, a ring, a registry, a dress—without thinking about what it is that we're agreeing to. You might feel certain that your guy is right for you, but before you move forward, you have to understand what commitment really entails. You must decide if you're ready to make a commitment at all before you can determine if you want to make one to him.

Defining Commitment

What do you think of when you hear the word *commitment*? Most of us think of pledging our lives to a person or a cause. But some of us also think of the alternate definition: confinement to jail or to an institution. If you are scared of commitment, take a moment to explore your feelings and decide if maybe you are confusing these two definitions.

Being committed to a person should not be a painful, confining experience. Rather, it is actually freeing because you break down the walls around you and let another person into your world, completely. You pledge to each other that you'll work together to overcome obstacles and stay together. You make a choice to be part of each other's lives, even though you know it will be hard work and that there will be moments when you struggle. You make this choice because you truly believe that the rewards of staying the course will be far greater than any temporary relief you get from giving up. Are you and your guy ready to make a commitment to each other?

Here is what commitment means to some people:

- Dr. Tom Merrill, a clinical and forensic psychologist, says commitment means "I share the same emotional, psychological, physical and spiritual space with my partner . . . for life. That space is no longer my space to do with as I wish. It is our space. And I don't get to clutter it up as if it is only mine."

- Bonnie Peltomaa, a writer for the *Mansfield News Journal* in Ohio, says "Commitment means that even when things don't go as we'd like, we stay together. Whether it's sickness, job layoffs, a slow economy, growing older, problems with the kids or just feeling out of sorts, we're going to hang in there. How we feel on any given day doesn't change our commitment to each other."

- Anna Pasternak, a writer for *The Daily Mail* in London says, "It is only when you have loved someone in the cold light of day, when you have felt the full force of their anger, when you have seen their capacity for humour or random acts of kindness, that you truly know what commitment means."

- "Commitment means you respond to someone with loyalty and love despite how you feel about them at the moment romantically."—*Cadence, age 29*

- "Sticking together even when times get tough, money gets tight, family members get sick, and kids get in trouble."—*Christopher, age 28*

- "It's not romance. Romance is superficial. It's fun and light and enjoyable. Commitment is hard work and often it's not fun at all."—*Sandra, age 46*

- "Commitment is saying 'I think I can' and continuing on even when you're so tired you don't want to take another step."— *Marie, age 27*

- "It's no different than when you pick a job. You don't leave the job just because it's tough now and then. If you believe the job is worthwhile, you stick with it, knowing that you're going to learn more, have greater satisfaction, and really succeed only through long-term dedication."—*Bethany, age 32*

When you get engaged, you are saying "I am ready and willing to make a commitment to you," and that means you are going to work to build a life with this person even when it's not easy. You are acknowledging that you will remain faithful to that person in times of doubt and temptation. The decision is not about a ring, or a dress, or a china pattern. It's the decision to take on a partner for the rest of your life. Are you really ready to do that?

> There are only two options regarding commitment. You're either IN or you're OUT. There's no such thing as life in-between.
>
> PAT RILEY

Are You Ready?

Friends, family, the media, relationship experts, and everyone in the world recognize how difficult it is to go through a breakup, but seldom do we hear about the fact that making a commitment and sticking with it is even harder. If you've determined your guy isn't right for you and that you need to say good-bye, by all means, do it. Do not hold on, thinking that things will get better if you get engaged, that somehow life will get easier. The truth is that it will only get harder.

But if you decide to stick with it and make things work, you'll need every ounce of energy and optimism you have. You will need an open mind, a strong will, and a positive outlook. Making a commitment to another person is a wonderful, exciting experience, but it's far too easy to focus on these care-free parts of it without really considering the enormity of the pledge you're making. You have to be ready, 100 percent, to make the pledge, because it's going to require your full dedication. If anything is standing in your way, preventing you from entering into this commitment with enthusiasm, you must expunge it from your life before moving forward.

Drop Your Baggage

Most of us are familiar with the word *baggage*—those beliefs and experiences that make us fearful that our own relationship won't work out. Perhaps your parents are divorced and it has given you a bad feeling about marriage, or maybe several men have been jerks to you in the past, so you now worry that eventually your guy will be a jerk to you too. Before you make a commitment, get rid of your baggage or at least learn to recognize when it is clouding your judgment. If you judge your guy harshly because of an experience you had in the past, it's not fair to him or good for your relationship. The two of you won't survive if you bring your baggage along and end up fighting or worrying needlessly because of it.

Bringing Baggage Along
Think about those things that are making you afraid of commitment. Your baggage might include:

- The fear that you'll get divorced someday, because you keep reading about how more than half of all marriages end in divorce.

- The fear that all men cheat, because your sister's husband cheated on her.
- The fear that your guy will dump you if you get fat, because one of your ex-boyfriends used to make this threat.
- The fear that if you get too emotional, your guy won't respect you, because that's what your mother always told you.
- The fear that you won't be able to stay faithful to him, because you cheated on another boyfriend in the past.
- The fear that your guy will leave you for a younger woman, because every man you work with has done the same thing to his wife.
- The fear that your relationship is doomed, because a magazine article you read says that young people today don't have what it takes to stay together for life.

Positive Thinking

Remind yourself that past experiences do not dictate your future. Like any other task you undertake, you won't be successful unless you enter it with a winning mind-set, one full of optimism and a strong will to succeed. So replace these negative thoughts with positive ones. Remind yourself that:

- Miserable couples get more front-page time than happy ones do. Most publications are looking for stories with a lot of drama, so they gravitate toward sensational accounts of breakup, murder, and disaster.
- You have power over the outcome of your relationship. By talking about major issues like money, children, sex, and what commitment means to both of you, you can avoid many of the pitfalls that cause other couples to split.

- According to an article by Julie Baumgardner, Director of First Things First, a research and advocacy organization dedicated to strengthening families, most men say they are happier married than they were when they were single, and many men really look forward to committing to a partner they love.
- Today, more than ever, research, programs, and counseling exist to help couples get through the hard times. You aren't on your own.
- There are examples everywhere of couples who have made it work and are glad they did.

Irrational fears and worries will keep you from entering into a commitment with the optimism and energy you need to make it work. Remind yourself that while it's often easy to fixate on bad experiences, you don't have to. You can model your life after the positive ones. You and your guy will stay together if you want to.

A Word on Doubt

It's important to remember that doubts and worries are not the same thing as baggage. Baggage is an irrational belief you bring in from outside the relationship. It's a thought or fear that has absolutely nothing to do with your relationship or your guy. Doubt, on the other hand, is a normal part of being human. Your doubts will stem from differences the two of you have and knowledge of how much work it takes to resolve them.

When you make a commitment to each other, you will have doubts. Your commitment is a pledge to resist them, to control them, and to love one another despite them. Make sure you fully understand the difference between doubts and baggage:

Baggage: You know that your sister had days when she wasn't feeling loving toward her husband, and she ended up divorcing him. Now you fear that your own off days will lead to the same fate for your relationship.

Doubt: You have days when you just don't feel loving toward your guy and you worry that they're signs he's not right for you. You remind yourself that having days when you're not "on" is normal, and you resolve to work through them.

Baggage: Your ex dumped you because he didn't want a woman who was so ambitious. Now, your guy is complaining that he doesn't get to see you often enough because you work so hard. You are worried that he's going to dump you too.

Doubt: Your guy's complaints worry you because you can't figure out a way to balance your relationship with your career. You tell him about your concerns and the two of you fight a little, but eventually you reach a compromise that makes you both happy.

Baggage: You are terrified of being hurt again because you have been hurt so often in the past. So you keep your emotions inside and refuse to share your full self with your guy.

Doubt: Whenever you say "I love you" to your guy, he says something silly in return. You worry that he doesn't really love you. As soon as you think about all the other ridiculous things he does to make you laugh, you realize that these responses are just part of his attempt to be your personal comedian.

Baggage: Your parents are divorced and you're convinced it runs in your family. You just don't know if you are going to have what it takes to hang in there through the tough times.
Doubt: Your parents are divorced and you know it's because being in a committed relationship isn't easy. You worry that you won't have what it takes to hang in there, but you vow to try anyway.

You might assume that when it's time to make a commitment, you just know the guy is exactly who you want in your life. But a big green light doesn't appear and tell you to keep on driving. Instead, a big yellow caution light blinks in your face and reminds you of all the doubts you have. Recognize that these doubts are normal but if you have the will and spirit to make the relationship work, you will succeed despite them.

The relationship between commitment and doubt is by no means an antagonistic one. Commitment is healthiest when it is not without doubt but in spite of doubt.

ROLLO MAY

Getting Engaged

Remember that people in loving, committed relationships don't agree on everything under the sun—including the timing of the proposal and the way they express their excitement about being engaged. Differences will pop up throughout the engagement process and sometimes you'll wonder if these differences are signs that he's not right for you. Like many other situations you'll face, working through these differences requires faith in the relationship, communication, and compromise.

The engagement is one of the first big situations where you'll expect him to want things to happen exactly the way you want them to, and of course they won't. If you're a traditional woman and want him to propose, be prepared to be flexible and to think the best even when things don't go exactly according to your plan.

His Timing

If you're feeling anxious waiting for him to get his act together and propose, remember that he has to work through all of his issues and fears too. A lot of factors determine when a guy proposes, and most of them aren't within your control. He has to feel ready, which means he has to view himself as an adult, have enough money to buy a ring, work through any doubts and worries he has, then create a plan and follow through with the proposal. He also has to feel pretty sure that you're going to say yes.

Inevitably, if he takes a long time to pop the question, you may start to wonder if he's ever going to propose at all or if maybe he doesn't really want to do it.

Or perhaps you have the opposite problem. You're just not ready to say yes and you're concerned he's going to propose too soon. Some women fear that a guy who proposes too early in the relationship is either desperate or he hasn't really thought it through. There are women on both sides of this timing issue, so remember if you're not thrilled with his timing, you're not alone.

That fact that your expectations differ from his is a real problem only if:

- He's made it clear he's never going to propose and you are in denial.
- You've made it clear to him that you don't want him to propose and he's in denial.
- You've been dating for several years, you're getting older, he knows you want to get married, and he still hasn't done it.
- He says things like, "I want to get engaged . . . but not to you."
- He is a serial monogamist, dating women for long periods of time, talking about engagement, but eventually dumping them when he gets bored.
- The two of you haven't talked at all about marriage, what it means to you, what your expectations are, and whether or not it's what you want.
- His friends ask you why you're wasting your time dating him.
- You notice he's not paying attention to you like he used to, or he's not treating you with love and respect, and yet you're still hoping he'll propose.
- Pressure from your family or his is influencing the timing of the proposal in a way that makes one or both of you uncomfortable.

If you don't agree on the timing, you can guess that you also might differ in opinion on the ring, the way he proposes, and some of the other details. If he doesn't have a psychic ability that enables him to pick out the perfect ring for you, that doesn't mean he's not the right guy. Go easy on him. He's surely doing the best he can. Being lifelong partners requires flexibility and compromise. Some of these early differences will test your ability to do so.

The Exciting Aftermath

Some experts say that often the enormity of the engagement doesn't really hit women until after it happens, whereas men have already worked through their issues, fears, anxieties, and they've even demonstrated their excitement to family and friends *before* they pop the question. Okay, so maybe that's giving guys too much credit, but there might be a little nugget of truth in this theory.

So don't be surprised if you both react to the engagement differently. Many women wake up the next morning feeling excitement and even relief. Guys wake up and pour themselves a cup of coffee. Women call their friends and family, send out e-mails, and notify coworkers that it's official. Guys receive calls from friends harassing them about giving up their freedom. After years of wondering who actually purchases bridal magazines, we buy a few. Then, we start planning the wedding. Guys pick up a brochure on Las Vegas and start planning the bachelor party. So expect your guy's reactions to be a little different than your own.

The truth is that many guys just don't seem as excited about the engagement and the wedding as women do. Here's what they have to say about it:

- "I love my fiancée dearly, but on my priority list, the wedding isn't even a close second to the NFL draft picks."—*Tom, age 31*
- "The wedding is her thing. Everyone knows that. My job is to stay out of the way and nod every time she asks a question." —*Chris, age 35*
- "I am pleasantly surprised that my girlfriend doesn't seem to be that into the whole engagement and wedding thing. People tell me that she'll change, but I don't believe it."—*Todd, age 27*
- "I would be happy if we just eloped. I don't understand all the hoopla over the process of getting married."—*Darren, age 25*
- "There are three guys on my basketball team who are about to get married. During practice, all they do is vent about how much their fiancées are driving them insane with all the wedding planning."—*Rob, age 31*
- "Women definitely make more out of the engagement than men do. You never hear a guy ask another guy how he proposed unless he's looking for a way to do it himself and he's too lazy to be creative."—*Erik, age 29*

Of course there are exceptions to the rule. Some men are excited and overwhelmed too. Some men are more into the wedding than women are. But assuming your guy isn't an exception, expect him to seem less excited than you are. You might worry that his less enthusiastic reaction is a sign he's not in love with you. But the truth is that many guys just don't talk about these events with the level of energy that women do. Part of your responsibility as a committed couple is to try to understand each other and accept the fact that you won't always react to situations in the same way.

Fights and Frights

It's not as if the process of getting engaged is all fun and excitement for women, and all angst for men. It's normal to get excited initially after the engagement, but then later face a number of fears and anxieties again about the commitment you are about to make. In other words, you might think that the hard work is done when you say yes to his proposal, but it's really just beginning.

The time after the engagement is a roller coaster ride of doubt, fear, and excitement. It is full of events and feelings that will challenge your commitment to your guy again and again. With marriage on the horizon, all his flaws will seem even bigger than they did before. You'll wonder, "Can I really live with that habit of his? I thought I could, but now that I might actually have to do it, I'm not so sure. Was I wrong about how much I love him? Am I really making the right decision?" You'll be forced to face yet again many of your biggest worries and fears.

Major Realizations

Other committed couples will talk to you about their married experience and force you to think about some of the less glamorous moments you'll share as a couple. Some of these thoughts might have already crossed your mind, but now they'll seem even more real and strange than they did before. You'll think things like:

- This is the man who is going to see me get old and develop varicose veins.
- This is the guy who will be with me when I'm lying naked on a birthing table.
- This is a guy who is going to have to help me through the death of my parents.
- This is a guy I'm going to have to love even when he gets age spots or goes completely bald.
- This is the guy I'm going to call my *husband.*
- Some day this guy and I will be really old people—together.
- This guy is going to be my partner for life. There's no more mystery surrounding who I will end up with. I have to make things work with him—with his job, with his paycheck, with his attitude, with his goals, with this man right here in front of me.

Normal Fears

If the first thing you feel after the proposal is sheer terror, then you might want to go back over some of the earlier chapters in this book to make sure he's the right guy for you. But if you start to feel a little scared after a couple of weeks pass, it's normal. For some women, fear is triggered by the flood of questions and congratulatory wishes. For others, it's triggered by the bridal shower or trying on the wedding dress or filling out the marriage license. There will be moments when you are almost sick to your stomach from the pressure of making this commitment. Surprisingly, many women go through the same thing, even those who are very happily married. Expect to have a variety of fears, some founded and some totally irrational. Things like:

- "Was his method of proposing good enough? Is the ring good enough? Did he get it out of a cereal box? Does it show he truly loves me or am I kidding myself?"
- "I don't want to be Mrs. [insert his last name]. It reminds me of his mother. Does that mean I might look like her when I get older too?"
- "What if our fights are just too much to bear? We're fighting more now. We fight about every wedding detail and he says I'm stressed out. What if these fights are a sign that it's all falling apart?"
- "What if he changes his mind? What if he calls me up tomorrow and tells me he made a grave mistake?"
- "What if his parents hate me? What if they kill me off by putting a pillow over my face when I sleep in the guest room?"
- "What if on the day of the wedding he tells me he thinks my dress is ugly or does something else to make me feel like I've made a big mistake and it's too late to turn back?"
- "What if he isn't the right guy for me? What if there's someone better out there and had I just looked for another week or another month, I would have found him?"
- "What if my parents really hate him and they aren't telling me?"
- "What if the fact that I'm scared about changing my name (or that I don't want to have bridesmaids, or that I don't want a big

wedding) is a sign that I don't really love him? What if I'm making the wedding different because I'm not really dedicated to going through the process with him?"

- "What if I never see my mom and dad again? What if this is it and I'm cutting them out of my life forever?"
- "What if that psychic was right back in eighth grade? What if my husband will die a tragic death and I'll end up a poor widow living on the streets?"

Rest assured every woman has complicated feelings and fears about getting married and they become even more real during the engagement. Some of these fears are just a product of the fact that women get married later today than they used to, so they have their own life, money, identity, and goals before they commit to a guy. Many of us fear we're going to be forced to give up this independent side of ourselves in marriage. The formal commitment process puts a lot of pressure on both people in the relationship, but if you love each other and you keep an open dialogue about how you're feeling, you'll work through these fears and be able to move forward with confidence.

Big Fights

Many couples also claim that they had more fights after they got engaged than they did before they got engaged. The added pressures of planning a wedding, dealing with family, and the emotion that accompanies making such a big commitment can make both of you want to flee. You might wonder if these arguments are a sign he's not right for you after all, but engagement squabbles are very normal. Here's what some women have to say:

- "I was so stressed out. If I asked Bill a question about the wedding and he didn't answer fast enough, I would yell at him and start crying."—*Anna, age 31*
- "We fought about everything from invitations to what schools our kids would go to even though we weren't planning on having kids for another five years."—*Samantha, age 28*
- "I would cry from all the stress and then call my mother and complain about John. The next day, I would be my happy self. My mom started to think I was going crazy."—*Erica, age 34*
- "Nothing was worse than when we went to get the marriage license and I had to write down the name I would take. We ended up having an argument in city hall about women's rights and what our roles were going to be in the marriage."—*Cindy, age 32*
- "Something about being engaged made us start to look at each other under a microscope. Every little thing I did, he would say, 'Ya know, I can't live with that forever.' One of our biggest fights was over who left the shaving cream on the edge of the tub and caused a rust ring."—*Jennifer, age 38*
- "The weeks before the wedding, I started reading all of these message boards to find out if the fights Dave and I were having were normal. I was relieved to hear so many women talking about the same thing."—*Theresa, age 33*

It is in your moments of decision that your destiny is shaped.

ANTHONY ROBBINS

Ready as Can Be

Never forget that you are the one who has control over your life and you have the sole right to decide whether or not you want to be with this man forever. We often feel pressure to do things that we don't want to do from family, friends, and the world around us. Sometimes these pressures are subtle and we don't even realize they are affecting us. Remind yourself before and after you get engaged that you are in control of this process and how it unfolds. You do not have to do things anyone else's way but your own. You can postpone the engagement, the wedding, or the whole relationship if you decide that's what you want to do. It's never too late. Watch out for outside pressures pushing you to do things you don't want to do, like:

- Your mother telling you that you're too picky and that you're too old to call it off
- Advertisements or programs that make weddings and marriage look more glamorous than they are

don't forget . . .

Don't forget, sometimes women do get engaged to the wrong man and the fears they are feeling after the engagement are very real and worth listening to. If you are experiencing abuse; he's cheating on you; someone coerced you into saying yes; or he's addicted to alcohol, drugs, or gambling, listen to your fears and call off your engagement.

- Parental or family pressure to have a huge wedding and invite everyone on the planet
- Your parents telling you they'll be embarrassed if you postpone the ceremony
- Your friends telling you how lucky you are and how you shouldn't give up a good thing
- Financial or other ties between the two of you
- Stories of people who aren't happy being single
- The engagement and wedding announcements of friends and classmates
- Your own artificial timeline of when things in your life are "supposed to happen"

Committing to the guy you love is a huge decision, one you have to make on your own. You and your guy both need to be dedicated fully to making the relationship last under all circumstances. If you aren't, you won't survive the inevitable challenges that will come your way. But if you are, you will experience satisfaction and companionship far greater than any short-term relationship can bring.

> My experience suggests that intimacy has two main components: RISK and COMMITMENT . . . Risk and commitment both require decisions.
>
> VICTOR L. BROWN, JR.

chapter ten

Go Ahead . . .
Flash That Finger

When we're kids, we imagine that we'll grow up, meet "The One," and live happily ever after. But once we've dated for a while, we learn that "The One" really means "THE-ONE-too-many-reasons-why-he-drives-me-crazy" or "THE-ONE-who-whistles-in-the-car-until-I-want-to-strangle-him." He's not this perfect being we expected him to be. He's a real person complete with strengths and weaknesses, flaws and adorable little idiosyncrasies. This fallibility is one of the reasons why we love him so much.

While you're dating a guy, you will wonder time and again what his place in your life should be. You'll evaluate him with a critical eye and imagine what your future would be like with him. Sometimes you might feel more comfortable when you're caught between loving him and leaving him. If you don't make a choice, you still have the freedom to dream and the comfort and happiness of having him near. But you can't have it both ways forever. Eventually you have to make a decision. You have to take all of the answers you've found and make peace with the ones you haven't. You have to determine once and for all if you are truly better off wed—to him.

First Things First

Have you studied your relationship, answered all the questions, and decided he's simply not right for you? If so, you now have a big task ahead of you: calling it off. As difficult as your decision may be, try to feel good about it or at least know that you will one day feel relieved. While there's no formulaic way to determine whether or not a man is "The One," it's often very easy to see that he's not. The problem is that most women see too late. They hang in there far longer than they should and they end up making the final decision after they are in a complicated marriage. So be proud of yourself. You've set your standards and you're making sure the men you date live up to them. If you need affirmation that your decision is right, keep in mind the following:

He Won't Change

He might agree to talk out problems or even go for counseling, but in the end, he simply will not change much, if at all. Thirty or forty years from now, he'll still be the way he is today. The things you fight about today will be there even when you're old and gray. So you have only two choices: live with him the way he is or don't.

It's Not Your Fault

Two people are often perfectly wonderful people on their own but horrible together. It's not your fault that the relationship doesn't work. You can't force it to work or make him fit with you if he doesn't. You can't bring him closer or make him love you more by changing yourself, your life, or your dreams. All you can do is let him go so you're free to meet people who fit into your life and make you happy.

It Wasn't a Waste of Time

Even if you dated him for five years or ten, you didn't date him in vain. Every relationship and every life experience teaches us a lesson that stays with us forever. While you might not see what you've learned right now, someday the benefits of what you've gone through will be apparent.

Break Up for Good

You will have moments after he's gone when you think you want him back again. You might even forget that he isn't right for you after being away from him for a while. Make a list of the reasons why he's not right for you. Refer to it whenever you are tempted to contact him again. Break up for good and move on.

Stay Busy

One of the hardest things about breaking up with a guy is filling the time that he took up in your life. Stay busy with friends. Take part in activities and go to places that don't remind you of him. The busier you are, the faster you will get over him, and the sooner you will realize that the decision you made is the right one.

Keep Your Eye on the Future

When you tell him good-bye, you might feel like your dating days are over. You might feel drained, tired, and even a little bit older. But remember that it is never too late to start over, and you will get your energy back. Once you get your spunk back, it will be clear to you in every way that moving on was the right decision.

The One for Life

Have you studied your relationship, answered all the questions, and decided that you think he is "The One"? Are you pretty sure that you want to spend your life with this guy? When you decide to make a commitment to the man you love, you pledge to overcome any remaining doubts you have, to push them aside and focus on making the relationship work. But staying positive and committed in a relationship is not always easy, and you'll often need an extra nudge to keep on going.

The exercise that follows will help you document why you love your guy. It will remind you that you didn't choose him because he's perfect. You chose him because you love him despite his imperfections. The questions correspond with previous chapters, and this list will help you organize your reactions to each chapter on one paper. When you're done, keep it with you. Put it in your nightstand drawer. Keep it by your side for years to come and read it whenever you feel you need a little reminder of why you want to make this relationship work.

Why Did You "Just Know" . . . or Not?

How did you and your guy meet? Maybe you adored him from the start or maybe he didn't win your heart until later in the game. But whatever your story is, write it down and focus on those elements that are unique. It's important to keep in mind those reasons why you decided to make this relationship happen in the first place.

But also think about what bugs you about the way you met. Maybe you didn't feel like the first date was romantic enough or maybe you hedged in the beginning and weren't sure about your feelings. Be honest with yourself. What were your earliest concerns?

Critical Question: How will you live with these concerns? What will you do to deal with them if they bug you again in the future?

How Does He Compare?

Compare him to all the other guys you know. Focus first on ways he is cuter or sweeter or more caring than they are. What does he have that they don't have? It's easy to get hung up on how he doesn't measure up to other men, but if you look again, you'll notice that he outshines them in many ways too.

Now think about the ways he falls short. Do you know a guy with a better body or a guy who makes more money?

Critical Question: How will you live with the fact that there is someone better out there in these particular areas? Will it affect you? How do you plan to deal with temptation?

How Does the Real Relationship Feel?

When the honeymoon period was over and you began to see him in a new, more genuine light, what is it that you liked about him? What positive discoveries did you make that kept you by his side? Make note of them.

Then think about what drove you crazy and made you want to flee. Why didn't you?

Critical Question: How will you live with these annoying things he does and how will you stay positive about the relationship despite them?

Why Are Your Fights Alright?

Think about the way you argue and fight. How do you reach an understanding? What does he do to show you that he forgives you? How have your fights brought you closer together?

Now think also about the things he does in a fight that drive you nuts. What issues remain unresolved regardless of how long and how frequently you argue?

Critical Question: How will you live with these issues if they are never resolved? How will you handle the things that drive you crazy about your fights in the future?

Why Do You Have Faith in Your Team of Two?

Recall the ways you've helped each other through tough situations. Why are you good as a team? How do you share responsibility and work together to resolve issues? What interests do you share? Think of the ways he shows you he cares.

Now, think of your team's biggest failures. In what areas does your team need to improve significantly?

Critical Question: How will you live with these weaknesses in your team? What will you do to handle them if they present a problem in the future?

What Gives Him a Hint of Hero?

How has he demonstrated that he has important qualities like patience and honesty? What does he do to show you he cares about you? What has he done to show you that he cares about other people too? Think of all the reasons you believe he's a genuinely good person.

Now, think about the ways he's not always quite so noble, the times when he falls short of the heroic ideal.

Critical Question: What makes you happy enough with him to stay by his side? In the areas where he's less than noble, how will you handle his shortcomings in the future?

How Will You Hold on to Yourself?

In what ways will you maintain your own life and independence once you're in a committed relationship? Why do you think he'll be a great addition to your life? How will he help you be an even better version of who you already are?

Now, think about those ways in which he stifles you a little bit. Or think about things you feel you need to change about yourself to make the relationship work.

Critical Question: What makes these changes tolerable? How will you balance your personal needs with his needs if they conflict down the road?

Why Is He the Right Fit?

What about him makes you happy? Think about how you feel when you're with him, how often you laugh, and how much the two of you talk. Note all of those things that make him the right fit.

Also, think about those ways in which he doesn't fit. Or note the differences you have with his family or friends.

Critical Question: Why can you live with this level of fit? How will you handle areas where you don't fit together just right? What will you do to prevent differences from coming between you?

Why Are You Both the Committing Kind?

Think about those ways in which you're both ready to commit to a long-term relationship. Note the conversations you've had about fidelity and trust.

Also recall any moments when you've been nervous and felt that you're not ready to commit or incidences that have made you call into question his degree of dedication.

Critical Question: What makes you think that you've both overcome your fears and you're ready to make a long-term commitment? How will you deal with any feelings that threaten your commitment to each other in the future?

Now Don't You Just Find Him Adorable?

There are so many times you want to hug your guy because he's so funny or kind and sweet. There are probably things he does that nobody else would even notice, things you love. Recount all the little reasons why you like him. From his smile to his style, make note of those things that make him worth holding on to that you didn't already cover above.

Critical Question: Do the good things about your guy far outweigh the bad? Are you tired of writing good things about him by now because you've written so many when answering the previous questions? Hopefully, the answer is yes!

The day will come when you don't remember why you're with your guy. You might be angry with him, feel like the relationship is falling apart, or be tempted to leave him. This list will be your positive reminder, that little voice that says, "You made a commitment. You love him. Now work at making it last."

A Bright Outlook

Commitment is hard work, but it isn't all drudgery. It's fun, exciting, and rewarding too. Why else would so many people choose to seal the deal every day with the person they love? At the time of the 2000 Census, over 120 million people in the United States (54.4 percent of people over fifteen) were married, and that number doesn't even take into account all of the people who have made less traditional commitments to one another or those who are widowed. So while it's important to keep a relationship in perspective, and expect challenges along the way, it's also important to stay positive and realize that you can make it work.

Encouraging News

There's no shortage of articles and stories that highlight the perils of being in a committed relationship. Accounts of celebrities and even everyday people showcase the emotional distress, battles over property, cheating, and many other problems that plague couples around the world. But not all of the news out there is bad news. There are many studies and reports that indicate that being in a committed relationship is good for you. Here are a few promising notes on couplehood:

- Many people argue that the well-known statistic "over 50 percent of marriages end in divorce" is based on faulty logic. They say that the real divorce rate is not so high. At the very least, there is evidence that divorce rates have declined modestly in recent years.
- Linda Waite, a University of Chicago sociology professor, has found that contrary to popular belief, committed couples have more sex and even more satisfying sex than their single counterparts do.
- Waite has also found that life expectancy and income are substantially higher for married couples.
- Studies cite the numerous emotional benefits of marriage, including companionship, a feeling of importance, a sense of belonging, and an improved sense of well-being overall.
- Dr. Ted Huston, Professor of Psychology and Human Ecology at the University of Texas found that people who take their time and get to know each other before they get married, also known as the "slow-motion group," have better prospects for remaining committed to one another long-term.
- Studies have concluded that women in happy relationships have better physical health than single, divorced, and widowed women.
- Some experts say that couples that get married later in life are less likely to get divorced.

Of course these benefits don't apply to women in abusive or unhappy relationships. There are no advantages to staying with a man who isn't right for you. But if your relationship is reasonably happy, you will reap these benefits.

The Best Is Yet to Come

In addition to the favorable studies and research, plenty of women in long-term relationships offer reasons why they are thrilled they took the plunge. Here are a few of the things you have to look forward to when you become a committed couple.

- "The best thing about being married to Mark is the fact that I always have a buddy right there to share my life with. It's such a great feeling to know that there's someone who cares about you by your side all the time."—*Kristin, age 37*
- "Frank and I never felt as close when we were dating as we do now. Something about making a formal commitment to one another made the bond more real."—*Ruth, age 44*
- "I love the fact that Joe remembers so many funny things that happened to us over the years. It makes me feel like we've really lived. We have this whole shared history to draw from when we talk."—*Sharon, age 64*
- "The truth is that I really enjoy knowing how to push his buttons. Sometimes it's funny. You don't really know how to make your husband squirm until you've been with him for a few years."—*Joy, age 33*
- "I love to work alone and spend time by myself but even when I'm doing my own thing, Todd is there if I need him. I feel like I

have the best of both worlds—my own life and a life with a great man."—*Nancy, age 36*

- "It's so nice to be able to plan for the future. I used to try to imagine where I would be ten years from now and there was always so much uncertainty. I still enjoy a level of spontaneity in my life, but it is nice to be able to picture the person who will be there with me down the road doing those spontaneous things."—*Elizabeth, age 38*

It's easy to get the impression from the media and even from other couples that committing to someone is a death sentence. Many stories lead us to believe that if we commit, we're in for a miserable breakup battle or years in an unhappy relationship. But there are plenty of studies and stories that paint a more optimistic picture of life as a couple. Obviously, no one benefits from being part of a relationship that is unhappy, abusive, or stifling. However, reasonably happy couples have plenty of reasons to celebrate.

A good marriage would be between a blind wife and a deaf husband.

HONORÉ DE BALZAC

Staying Happy

But how do couples stay happy if they are living every day with peeves, doubts, and annoyances brought on by their partner? This question is one that researchers, psychologists, and real couples spend plenty of time trying to answer. Some argue that it's impossible to keep a relationship going today, but many couples who've made it work for years say it's not really as hard as you think. There are moments when it's a lot of work and times when it tests your patience, but in the end, you can stay happy if you stay focused on the commitment you've made.

> More marriages might survive if the partners realized that sometimes the better comes after the worse.
>
> DOUG LARSON

By the Book

What are those keys to lasting happiness in your relationship? Is it romantic dinners for two or financial security? Is it couples counseling for everyone? While there's no magic pill or one-size-fits-all answer, these basic tenants can help you and your guy stick together through the good times and the bad.

Keep Your Own Life in Order

For a relationship to work, each person in it must be happy. If you're feeling depressed or overwhelmed because of events in your own life at work or at home, your negative attitude will affect your partner. So the first step in keeping your marriage happy is keeping yourself happy.

Talk (Even If He Doesn't Want To)

All happy couples stress the need for communication. Find time every day to talk to each other about the mundane and the important issues in your lives. Don't stop communicating, ever, even if you get so busy you barely have time to shower. Make talking to one another your top priority.

Set Ground Rules

Make sure you both know what you expect from each other and how it will make you feel if the other person does something to hurt you. Tell each other what type of affection you need and how you define loyalty. Don't wait until something bad happens in the relationship to make your standards and expectations known.

Have Realistic Expectations

Make sure that you both realize that you will face obstacles as a couple. Acknowledge to each other that staying focused on the relationship can be tough, especially when life is busy and pressures at work or at home are mounting. Don't expect perfection from one another. Be realistic in what you expect. Also, talk to each other about what you need. Make it clear to him what will make you happy and why. Don't leave it up to him to read your mind.

Take One for the Team

Don't be too proud to say "I'm sorry" first. Being in a committed relationship means you have to be the sucker sometimes. You have to be the one to cry and ask for forgiveness.

The easiest way to tone down a fight is to say "I'm sorry." Try to acknowledge one another's viewpoint even when you're angry and annoyed.

Look for the Positive

Interpret each other's remarks and moods as positively as you can. Don't look for reasons to be annoyed or reasons to feel let down. Focus on the reasons to be happy in the relationship. If you're going to keep tabs, keep them on what your partner does right. If you look for reasons to be angry with each other, you'll find them.

Don't Look Back

Once you commit to one another, push out of your mind all of the what-ifs and could-have-beens. Look forward. Stay focused on the future, the decision you've made, and what you can do to make the relationship the best it can be.

Real-World Wisdom

In addition to these universal guidelines, think about those little things that will work for you and your guy. What is unique about your relationship and what can you both do to make it last? Here are a few suggestions offered by real couples:

- "You have to keep having fun. You won't always be able to enjoy life in the same ways you did when you first met, but you have to find new ways to have a blast together."—*Lisa, age 40*

- "You have to make time to talk without any other distractions. Don't assume you'll fit it in. Schedule a walk each week or a dinner where you can chat about your life together."—*Jill, age 36*
- "Stop paying attention to what other women have. Sure, her husband might clean the bathroom, but look at his big forehead. Would you really want to be married to that?"—*Christine, age 29*
- "Don't cheat, ever. You can never really forgive someone for destroying a relationship that takes years to build. Why would you even want to?"—*Maria, age 45*
- "Don't let your in-laws rule your life. It might be easier said than done, but you have to make the decisions based on what is good for you as a couple, not good for them."—*Trish, age 34*
- "If you let your children take precedence over your marriage, it will fall apart. Obviously they are important, but you have to nurture your relationship too."—*Patricia, age 40*
- "Tell the truth about the big issues—money, sex, kids, health—but lie like hell about how the other person looks."—*Heather, age 43*

Some people ask the secret of our long marriage. We take time to go to a restaurant two times a week. A little candlelight, dinner, soft music and dancing. She goes Tuesdays, I go Fridays.

HENNY YOUNGMAN

You never really stop trying to iron out all the kinks in a relationship—after all, if you succeeded, the darn thing would be flat and that wouldn't be much fun. But if you both remain dedicated to each other and to the commitment you've made, your relationship will thrive. Eventually you'll become so intertwined that you even start to look like each other. (But don't worry . . . he's the ugly twin.) Of course you'll endure nightmarish moments that test the relationship from every angle. But you'll also have plenty of wonderful times and moments to celebrate. You never stop learning about each other and every new nugget of information brings you closer together. Each battle, each difference, and each fun time solidifies the bond between you.

> Love seems the swiftest but it is the slowest of all growths. No man or woman really knows what perfect love is until they have been married a quarter of a century.
>
> MARK TWAIN

Conclusion

You've answered every question, even the really tough ones. You've analyzed your guy inside out and upside down, held him up to the light, and peered at him through a magnifying glass. You've done your best to predict what kind of impact he'll have on your future. But yet, you're still just not sure. Is he "The One"? Can he really be it?

You're still waiting for a sign, for the golden answer. But you now suspect that maybe there is no golden answer. You wonder if maybe you're trying to solve a puzzle that is not completely solvable. So you think about your guy again and what you love about him. Then you finally accept the fact that there is no absolute truth, no one way to know he's it, no formula, no psychic revelation, no astrology report, no tarot reading, no DNA results, no lie detector test, no flashing sign, no billboard, no light in the sky, no bolt of lightening, no visitation from beyond, no moment of complete and utter clarity where all of your questions are answered and your future is laid out before you.

Choosing a life partner is the very last leap of faith left on earth, one that you have to take on your own. But you can do it! You and you alone can draw upon all the knowledge and experience you have and decide once and for all if you truly are better off wed.

References

Atkins, Dale. Psychologist and Relationship Expert for *www.wedding channel.com.* Quoted in Kim Campbell, "I Do, I Don't, I'm Not Sure: Modern Wedding Jitters." *The Christian Science Monitor,* May 5, 2005.

Baumgardner, Julie. Director of First Things First. Quoted in Julie Baumgardner, "Determining If a Guy is Really Marriage Material." *Chattanooga Times Free Press,* July 11, 2004.

Gottman, Dr. John. Professor of Psychology, University of Washington. *www.johngottman.com.* Quoted in Shia Kapos, "Curtailing Criticism Can Help a Couple." *Chicago Tribune.* July 21, 2004. Also Quoted in Kathleen Kelleher, "Birds & Bees: Dissecting the Dysfunctions that Lead Down the Path to Divorce." *The Los Angeles Times,* September 18, 2000.

Hazen, Cindy. Cornell University Psychologist. Quoted in Patricia Wen, "In Science, Love Now Has a Reality Check." *The Boston Globe,* February 14, 2001.

Huston, Dr. Ted. Professor of Psychology and Human Ecology at the University of Texas at Austin. Quoted in Kaja Perina, "Courting Disaster: Can You Predict Which Marriages Will Last?" *Psychology Today* 36, no. 3 (May 1, 2003): 11. Also Quoted in: Carey, Benedict. "The Brain In Love." *The Los Angeles Times.* December 16, 2002, sec. 6.

Luo, Shanhong, and Eva C. Klohen. Assortative "Mating and Marital Quality in Newlyweds: A Couple Centered Approach." *Journal of Personality and Social Psychology* 88. no. 2 (2005): 304-326.

MaCrae C.N., K.A. Alnwick, A.B. Milne, A.M. Schloerscheidt. "Person Perception Across the Menstrual Cycle: Hormonal Influences on Social-Cognitive Functioning." *Psychological Science* 13, no. 6 (November 2002): 532-36.

Marazziti, Donatella, and Domenico Canaleb. "Hormonal Changes When Falling in Love." *Psychoneuroendocrinology* 29, no. 7 (August 2004): 931-36.

Merrill, Dr. Tom. Clinical and Forensic Psychologist. *www.tommerrill.com.* Quoted in Dr. Tom Merrill, "The Art of Unlimited Relationships," Cox News Service. March 30, 2005.

Pasternak, Anna. "Generation Ex," *Daily Mail*, September 2, 2004, first edition.

Peltomaa, Bonnie J. "What the World Needs Now Really is Love," *Mansfield News Journal*, January 29, 2005.

Potts, Ken, "Love at First Sight Isn't Enough to Sustain a Happy Marriage." *Chicago Daily Herald*, November 6, 2004.

Ramirez Jr., Artemio and Michael Sunnafrank. "At First Sight: Persistent Relational Effects of Get-Acquainted Conversations." *Journal of Social and Personal Relationships* 21, no. 3 (2004): 361-79.

U.S. Census 2000 Brief, "Marital Status," *www.census.gov* (accessed October 2003).

Waite, Linda. University of Chicago sociology professor. Quoted in William Poter, "Marriage is Good for You In Lots of Ways, Studies Find." *The Denver Post.* February 6, 2001.

Index

A

abusive relationships, 103–109
addictions, 107–108
adoration, 78–79
alone time, 129–131, 173
anxiety. *See* fears
arguments. *See* fights/fighting
attention, diverted, 62–63
attraction: instant, 2–3; lack of initial, 9–10; one-sided, 15–16; physical, 4–5

B

baggage, getting rid of, 203–205
balanced relationships, 86–87
best friend, boyfriend of, 46–47
boyfriend: annoying habits of, 59; behavior of, in beginning of relationship, 77–79; of best friend, 46–47; comfort with, 41, 180–181; comparing your, to other guys, 35–55; determining if he has right fit, 177–183, 219–228; disagreements with. *see* fights/fighting; lack of attention from, 62–63; positive discoveries about, 72–74; realistic expectations about, 70–72; staying with wrong, 51–53; treatment of you by, 150–154; trying to change, 20–21, 40, 52–53, 183–186
bravery, 153–154
breaking up: barriers to, 188–194; deciding on, 220–222; pain of, 51; recognizing time for, 53

C

caring, 135, 150–151
celebrities, 7
celebrity type, 33
challenges: everyday-type, 119–123; major, 123–129
character: importance of good, 133–142; tests of, 145–154
charmers, 32
chemistry, 4, 16; *See also* attraction
comedians, 33
comfort level, 41, 180–181
commitment: *See also* engagement; benefits of, 228–231; deciding on, 222–228; defining, 199–202; meaning of, 115–118; mixed feelings about, 155–164, 174–175; questioning, 194–197, 205–207; readiness for, 202–205; signs of, 113–114
communication: honest, 61–62; importance of, 173, 233; lack of, 88–89
comparisons: are normal, 49–51; benchmarks used for, 42–48; between men, 35–55, 224; positive, 53–55; recognizing unhealthy, 36–48
confidence, 28
conflicts. *See* fights/fighting
contempt, 88
couplehood: balancing single self with, 172–175; gains from, 167–172; meaning of, 115–118; signs of, 111–114; tests of, 119–129
courting phase. *See* honeymoon period
criticism, 88, 93

D

death of loved one, 193–194
decision making, 219–228
defensiveness, 88
disagreements. *See* fights/fighting
doubt, 205–207
driving issues, 121

E

80 percent rule, 186–188
engagement, 199–200; *See also* commitment; aftermath of, 210–212; fears and anxiety after, 212–218; outside pressures about, 217–218; timing of, 208–210
"enough" rule, 142–144
envy, of other women's boyfriends, 46–47
ex-boyfriend, comparing current boyfriend to, 45
expectations, realistic, 70–72, 233

F

family, as role models, 146–147
family pressures, to stay in relationship, 189–190
family stress, 124–125
fantasy man, 27

fashion sense, 28–29

fears: about being in relationship, 156–163; about breaking up, 191–192; after engagement, 213–215; unfounded, 72–74, 170, 172

fights/fighting, 60, 81–109, 225; after engagement, 215–216; apologizing in, 233–234; destructive, 87–89; goodwill during, 83–85; letting go of, 102–103; minor, 60; vs. positive interactions, 86–87; positives of, 82–83; pushing buttons during, 101; reasons for, 92–97; red flags in, 103–109; reducing, 97–100; style of, 85–86, 90–91

financial dependence, 190–191

first dates: judgments made on, 26–31; strange behaviors on, 29–31

first impressions, mistaken, 14–15

fit. See right fit

friends: beginning as, 10–11; as character test, 145–146; comparing boyfriend to, 48; less time with, 158–159; meeting new, 169

fun, 179–180

G

growing up, fear of, 161–163

H

habits: annoying, 59; loveable, 182–183

happiness, 179–180, 231–234

health problems, 125–126, 193–194

honesty, 61–62, 136, 151

honeymoon period, 57–58; lack of, 74–80; transitioning out of, 58–69

household issues, 120

hygiene, 78

I

ideal man, 27

independence, 168–169; fear of losing, 157–158

indifference, 77

initial attraction. See attraction

in-laws, 189

inner-circle test, 145–146

insecurities, 28, 95

instincts, paying attention to, 24–26

intellectual type, 32–33

interests, shared, 73–74

J

jealousy, 94

job stress, 122–123

job test, 147

just a friend test, 148

L

limits, setting your, 68–69

listener type, 33

long-term relationships: See also commitment; relationships; different formulas for, 16, 17; initial attraction and, 2–7, 16; positive views of, 228–231; staying happy in, 231–234

love: in the movies, 7; recognizing true, 1–2, 8, 16–24

love at first sight, 2–7, 15–16

loyalty, 136–137, 152

M

manners, 29–31, 78

marriage: See also commitment; fears and anxiety about, 212–218; mixed feelings about, 163–164; positives of, 228–231; staying happily, 231–234

masochists, 23

meltdowns, 93–94

men: See also boyfriend; comparing your man to other, 35–55; reaction of, to getting engaged, 210–212; salesmen strategies used by, 32–33; typical qualities of, 70–71

misinterpretations, 94

money issues, 126–127, 190–191

moves, 124, 193

movie test, 148–149

N

needs, sacrificing own, 116–117, 138–139, 154

O

obligation, 192

One, The. See true love

one-sided attraction, 15–16

opinions, honest expression of, 61–62

opportunities: fear of missed, 160–161; new, 169–170

P

past: letting go of, 162–163, 234; selective memory about, 165–167

patience, 60–61, 137–138, 153

perfection, vs. good enough, 142–144
personal interests, 173
personality similarities, 4
personality traits, 133–142; *See also* character
pessimists, 21–22
phone calls, as indicator, 12–13
physical abuse, 104–106
physical attraction. *See* attraction
positive qualities, focusing on, 53–55
positive thinking, 204–205, 234
preferences, having similar, 28–29
privacy, 159–160
profession, 147
proposals: *See also* engagement; timing of, 208–210

Q

qualities: "enough" rule for, 142–144; important, 133–142, 225–226; loveable, 182–183

R

rational thinkers, 17–18
real you, 180–181
reconciliations, after fights, 84–85
red flags, 103–109
relationships: *See also* couplehood; long-term relationships; abusive, 103–109; balanced, 86–87; barriers to ending, 188–194; beginning as friendships, 10–11; changes in, after honeymoon period, 58–69; ending, 53, 220–222; honeymoon period of, 57–58; making decisions about, 219–228; off days in, 129–131; positive discoveries in, 72–74; realistic expectations about, 70–72, 233; real-life beginnings to, 7–11; red flags in, 103–109; staying in wrong, 51–53, 194–197; wrong reasons to start, 75–77
rescuers, 44
responsibility, sharing, 62–64
responsible behavior, 152–153
right fit: 80 percent rule for, 186–188; defining, 177–178, 184; determining if your guy has, 178–183, 219–228; forcing a, 183–186; tests of, 194
rituals, new, 171
role models, 146–147
romantics, 18–19

S

second chances, 24–31; checklist for giving, 31, 34; when not to give, 24–26
self-blame, 221
self-confidence, 39
selflessness, 116–117, 138–139, 154
settling, 194–197
sharing, with partner, 170
similarities, discovering, 74
single self, 155–175, 226; balancing, with couplehood, 172–175; fears about losing, 156–163; missing your, 155–156; mixed feelings about, 163–164; selective memory about, 165–167; sharing, with partner, 167–172
social type, 33
soul mates, 3
space, needing own, 159–160
stonewalling, 88–89
story-telling tests, 149–150
strange behaviors, 29–31
strangers, comparing your guy to, 42–43
strengths, enhancing, 181–182
supportive behavior, 117–118, 135–136, 151

T

table manners, 29–31
tastes, 28–29
telephone calls, 12–13
temptations, 128–129
time issues, 127–128
true love, recognizing, 1–2, 8, 16–24
twosomes. *See* couplehood

U

unselfish behavior, 116–117, 138–139, 154

V

vacations, 121–122
verbal abuse, 106–107

W

wandering eye. *See* comparisons
wheeler and dealer type, 32
women: men's pet peeves about, 71–72; reaction of, to getting engaged, 210–212
wrong guy: settling for, 194–197; ways to tell if your with the, 36–41

About the Author

ALISON JAMES is an expert in relationship and lifestyle issues affecting young women today. She combines her unique background in public policy with personal experience to create books that entertain, empower, and inspire women. A graduate of Princeton University's Woodrow Wilson School and the London School of Economics, James has researched a variety of policy issues including how the media influences the female psyche and personal development in a number of arenas.

James began her career as an advisor and mentor to young women in her hometown of Johnson City, New York. Now her work stretches internationally. Her previous works include *The 10 Women You'll Be Before You're 35* (May 2005) and the hit breakup survival guide *I Used to Miss Him . . . But My Aim is Improving* (April 2004). They have been featured in *Maxim, Woman's Own, Complete Woman, More Magazine, USA Weekend, The Ladies Home Journal, The Wall Street Journal, The New York Post, The London Daily Mirror,* and more. She has appeared on VH1's "Most Awesomely Bad Breakup Songs," the Soap Network's "Soap Talk," the CBS Evening News, Cinemax, Nashville's "Talk of the Town," and in several nationally televised commercials. She has been interviewed on over 200 radio stations in North America, Europe, and Australia.

Alison James is also the Director of Finance for A&E Television Networks and The History Channel. She lives in New York City.